Letters written during a residence in England. Translated from the French of Henry Meister. ... Together with a letter from the Margravine of Anspach to the author.

Jacques-Henri Meister

ECCO

PRINT EDITIONS

Eighteenth Century
Collections Online
Print Editions

Gale ECCO Print Editions

Relive history with *Eighteenth Century Collections Online*, now available in print for the independent historian and collector. This series includes the most significant English-language and foreign-language works printed in Great Britain during the eighteenth century, and is organized in seven different subject areas including literature and language; medicine, science, and technology; and religion and philosophy. The collection also includes thousands of important works from the Americas.

The eighteenth century has been called "The Age of Enlightenment." It was a period of rapid advance in print culture and publishing, in world exploration, and in the rapid growth of science and technology – all of which had a profound impact on the political and cultural landscape. At the end of the century the American Revolution, French Revolution and Industrial Revolution, perhaps three of the most significant events in modern history, set in motion developments that eventually dominated world political, economic, and social life.

In a groundbreaking effort, Gale initiated a revolution of its own: digitization of epic proportions to preserve these invaluable works in the largest online archive of its kind. Contributions from major world libraries constitute over 175,000 original printed works. Scanned images of the actual pages, rather than transcriptions, recreate the works *as they first appeared.*

Now for the first time, these high-quality digital scans of original works are available via print-on-demand, making them readily accessible to libraries, students, independent scholars, and readers of all ages.

For our initial release we have created seven robust collections to form one the world's most comprehensive catalogs of 18th century works.

Initial Gale ECCO Print Editions collections include:

History and Geography
Rich in titles on English life and social history, this collection spans the world as it was known to eighteenth-century historians and explorers. Titles include a wealth of travel accounts and diaries, histories of nations from throughout the world, and maps and charts of a world that was still being discovered. Students of the War of American Independence will find fascinating accounts from the British side of conflict.

Social Science

Delve into what it was like to live during the eighteenth century by reading the first-hand accounts of everyday people, including city dwellers and farmers, businessmen and bankers, artisans and merchants, artists and their patrons, politicians and their constituents. Original texts make the American, French, and Industrial revolutions vividly contemporary.

Medicine, Science and Technology

Medical theory and practice of the 1700s developed rapidly, as is evidenced by the extensive collection, which includes descriptions of diseases, their conditions, and treatments. Books on science and technology, agriculture, military technology, natural philosophy, even cookbooks, are all contained here.

Literature and Language

Western literary study flows out of eighteenth-century works by Alexander Pope, Daniel Defoe, Henry Fielding, Frances Burney, Denis Diderot, Johann Gottfried Herder, Johann Wolfgang von Goethe, and others. Experience the birth of the modern novel, or compare the development of language using dictionaries and grammar discourses.

Religion and Philosophy

The Age of Enlightenment profoundly enriched religious and philosophical understanding and continues to influence present-day thinking. Works collected here include masterpieces by David Hume, Immanuel Kant, and Jean-Jacques Rousseau, as well as religious sermons and moral debates on the issues of the day, such as the slave trade. The Age of Reason saw conflict between Protestantism and Catholicism transformed into one between faith and logic -- a debate that continues in the twenty-first century.

Law and Reference

This collection reveals the history of English common law and Empire law in a vastly changing world of British expansion. Dominating the legal field is the *Commentaries of the Law of England* by Sir William Blackstone, which first appeared in 1765. Reference works such as almanacs and catalogues continue to educate us by revealing the day-to-day workings of society.

Fine Arts

The eighteenth-century fascination with Greek and Roman antiquity followed the systematic excavation of the ruins at Pompeii and Herculaneum in southern Italy; and after 1750 a neoclassical style dominated all artistic fields. The titles here trace developments in mostly English-language works on painting, sculpture, architecture, music, theater, and other disciplines. Instructional works on musical instruments, catalogs of art objects, comic operas, and more are also included.

The BiblioLife Network

This project was made possible in part by the BiblioLife Network (BLN), a project aimed at addressing some of the huge challenges facing book preservationists around the world. The BLN includes libraries, library networks, archives, subject matter experts, online communities and library service providers. We believe every book ever published should be available as a high-quality print reproduction; printed on-demand anywhere in the world. This insures the ongoing accessibility of the content and helps generate sustainable revenue for the libraries and organizations that work to preserve these important materials.

The following book is in the "public domain" and represents an authentic reproduction of the text as printed by the original publisher. While we have attempted to accurately maintain the integrity of the original work, there are sometimes problems with the original work or the micro-film from which the books were digitized. This can result in minor errors in reproduction. Possible imperfections include missing and blurred pages, poor pictures, markings and other reproduction issues beyond our control. Because this work is culturally important, we have made it available as part of our commitment to protecting, preserving, and promoting the world's literature.

GUIDE TO FOLD-OUTS MAPS and OVERSIZED IMAGES

The book you are reading was digitized from microfilm captured over the past thirty to forty years. Years after the creation of the original microfilm, the book was converted to digital files and made available in an online database.

In an online database, page images do not need to conform to the size restrictions found in a printed book. When converting these images back into a printed bound book, the page sizes are standardized in ways that maintain the detail of the original. For large images, such as fold-out maps, the original page image is split into two or more pages

Guidelines used to determine how to split the page image follows:

• Some images are split vertically; large images require vertical and horizontal splits.
• For horizontal splits, the content is split left to right.
• For vertical splits, the content is split from top to bottom.
• For both vertical and horizontal splits, the image is processed from top left to bottom right.

LETTERS

WRITTEN DURING A RESIDENCE IN

ENGLAND,

TRANSLATED FROM THE FRENCH

OF

HENRY MEISTER,

CONTAINING

MANY CURIOUS REMARKS UPON ENGLISH MANNERS AND
CUSTOMS, GOVERNMENT, CLIMATE, LITERATURE, THE-
ATRES, &c. &c &c.

TOGETHER WITH

A LETTER FROM THE MARGRAVINE OF
ANSPACH TO THE AUTHOR

LONDON

PRINTED FOR T N LONGMAN AND O REES, NO 39, PA-
TERNOSTER-ROW

1799

TO

HIS SERENE HIGHNESS

CHRISTIAN FREDERIC CHARLES ALEXANDER,

MARGRAVE

OF

BRANDENBURG, ANSPACH, BAYREUTH, &c. &c. &c

May it please your Serene Highness,

RELYING for pardon on the known benignity of Your disposition, I have presumed, without permission, to place this translation of M. Meister's *Souve-*

nirs de ses Voyages en Angleterre under Your Protection, and to introduce it to the public with Your August Name prefixed to it.

And I have been the rather induced to use this liberty, because Your Serene Highness hath, in a particular manner, protected my author, who, on that account, however he may be dissatisfied with my manner of naturalizing him with the English nation, cannot but approve of the Patron I have assigned him in this country.

There were other reasons which irresistibly prevailed with me in this respect, as they must do with every sincere

cere lover of this country; amongst these are, the honour Your Serene Highness hath done it by making Your residence in it, and the choice You have made of an English Lady for Your consort, (a Lady whose least distinction it is that she is descended from the most ancient line of English nobility;) the former being as convincing a proof of Your attachment to the cause of liberty, as the latter appeareth to be of Your great judgment and discernment : these, Sir, are claims which intitle You to every mark of respect from English people; amongst the last of the literary body of whom, though amongst the foremost of the admirers of Your many Princely Vir-

tues,

tues, I beg leave to subscribe myself, with the utmost deference, and the profoundest veneration,

May it please Your Serene Highness,

Your most devoted,

most obedient, and

most humble servant,

THE TRANSLATOR.

CONTENTS.

LET-

ful in their imitation of the British constitution —English loyalty —English actors—Mrs Siddons—Mrs Kemble—Mrs Brooks—Mrs Bannister—Edwin —English stage how controuled—remark upon it —Destruction of the Bastille, a pantomime upon the English stage —Caricatures of the French king —The author attends debates in parliament —Eulogium on Mr Pitt —British House of Commons and French National Assembly compared

LETTER IV —Page 35

OF THE BRITISH CONSTITUTION—OF POPULAR ELECTIONS

The author a professed admirer of the British constitution and why —Criminal jurisprudence—defective in England—its code depraved throughout Europe.—Criminals in England too frequently escape justice—Barrington instanced —Common law of England perverted.—Trial by jury—wherein justice may be defeated by it —National representation far from compleat in England—wherein the French mistake in this respect —The English sufficiently represented in the House of Commons to answer every purpose —House of Lords—wisdom of such a barrier betwixt the prerogative of the Crown and the licentiousness of the popular part of the constitution —The author thinks the English nation too wise not to profit by the dangerous example of France in attempts at revolution—wise remark of a Jew, upon the subject.—Idea of the British constitution

LET.

sity of character, the English only describable indi-
vidually.—French women neglect to nurse their own
children.—Invitation to the author

The author highly gratified by her ladyship's correction—did not presume to give a description of England, but of his own sensations—his defence against
the charge of having said the English ladies were
aukward.—Some handsome compliments paid to her
ladyship.

LETTER VII —Page 91

OF SHAKSPEARE.

His character not now to be decided on—and by no
means in France —The superiority of the English
stage as little to be determined —Rule for judging of
the particular merits of Shakspeare, Corneille and
Racine—the plots of Corneille and Racine more regular, but Shakspeare's more productive of theatrical
effect—what Voltaire has said on the subject —Difference of English and French dramatic productions,
wherein it consists —Comparison of Shakspeare with
Racine.—In what respect French translations of
Shakspeare may prove prejudicial.—Shakspeare could
not have succeeded better had he been acquainted
with the Greek and Roman authors. Danger of
transferring theatrical beauties of one country to another.—Hints might be borrowed from the English
stage by the French writers—Voltaire has given the
example

LET-

LETTER VIII.—Page 102

OPINION OF THE ENGLISH NATION ON ROUSSEAU'S SOCIAL CONTRACT

Why the English do not approve of it —No society without government —Certain rights existed before the primitive compact —How far the rights of a people extend—what is meant by the people Union of interests and power —Power subject to natural influences —General will of a people not to be fully represented —Sovereignty of the people—its effects—not like the phœnix reviving from its ashes —Power, if unjustly exercised, destructive of itself —A proper respect due to ancient institutions —Interests and duty of the sovereign power.—All good progressive—how to render it durable.

LETTER IX —Page 112.

MORE OF OLD FASHIONED POLITICS, BEING A CONTINUATION OF THE SUBJECT OF THE FOREGOING LETTER.

Power and liberty universally wished for—in what liberty consists —Law a moral force—liable to be counteracted by other forces, physical as well as moral—its execution must be somewhere confided—difficulty where to place it—not with the army—not with the clergy—and why—not with the people at large, and for what reason —The democratic a most absurd and monstrous form of government—inconveniences attending it —Hereditary privileges and honours ought to be continued—advantages of them Why the monarchical has been the prevailing form —

Re

Representative government.—Influence of riches and poverty on government—Wny Europe has been less disturbed during the last than in former centuries

WHAT A TRAVELLER OUGHT TO BE.

Greater difficulty in characterizing an individual than a country—why the generality of travellers fail in the attempt—whether the native or stranger is best qualified to describe a country —A traveller should note his first ideas, but not hazard them until well considered —Ancient and modern nations how to be studied.—French nation better known by dramatic exhibitions, and productions of tne press, than by religion, laws, and manners —Difference discoverable in Spanish, Italian, and English writers —Distinguishing characteristic of the French authors —Will the new French constitution alter the French character, or the character the constitution, after a trial of twenty years?

OF THE ENGLISH CLIMATE—PRESENT STATE OF ENGLAND WITH RESPECT TO THE FRENCH REVOLUTION.

The author's second visit to England --Candour in the relation of travellers an excuse for misrepresentations —Opinions compared to mistresses—some make a like discovery with respect to opinions as a certain lover did of his mistress—the lover's acknowledgment of his discovery —The manners and disposi-

sitions

tions of a people vary according to climate and food —
English climate described—the Marquis de Caraccioli's remark upon it   A French writer's observation on the author of the Night Thoughts —Effects
of climate on the English character —Seacoal contributes to the fogs of London —Why the Londoners
rise late in the morning, and rejoice when they
catch a glimpse of the sun —English poets in greater
number, and more excellent than English painters—
the reason of it —Diet and its effects   The first
Lord Clive—English government had its apprehensions on the revolution taking place in France—
what will be the means of saving it from the mischievous effects of democratic principles —*Liberty*
and *equality* magical words —Different sentiments of
different classes of the English people with respect to
revolution —The Revolution Influenza has taken
place in England —Tom Paine and his Rights of
Man—he is compared to the Abbé Sieyes.—Democratic publications —Democratic newspapers.—
All the daily prints give accounts of the French proceedings —The English still venerate their own constitution, but from the increase of taxes do not idolize
it as formerly —Two circumstances influence revolutionary principles —The author's reasons why a
revolution is not likely to take place in England

LETTER XII —Page 163

OF SEACOAL, AND ITS MORAL AND PHYSICAL
EFFECTS

Introductory observation —Coals make a more lasting
and

and stronger fire than wood—more necessary in England from the great humidity of the atmosphere —
Physical advantages and disadvantages of coal-fires—
their moral influence—instanced in the good sense
and humanity of the higher classes—in the decency
and good order which obtain amongst the lowest
classes of the English nation—in the boxing matches
of the mob, which are subject to a point of honour
never infringed upon —Election riots no exception,
the *majesty of the people* being then in a state of
frenzy —Romeo and Juliet, the first English tragedy
the author saw acted—Mrs. Esten played Juliet for
the first time—remarks upon her performance—the
author watches its effects on the audience —Passions, in a French audience, discovered in a different
manner —The author pays particular attention to a
young lady—she appeared to be unaffected, but suddenly faints away—this imputed to the fumés of seacoal —Good sense depends on a right organical formation of the human body.—Phrase used by Horace
to denote a man of wit —A correcter and purer taste
prevails in the Greek and Roman than in the English
authors.

LETTER XIII —Page 177

SECOND DESCRIPTION OF LONDON

The author's former visit of no continuance and during
fine weather—this time otherwise.—Immense extent
of London—its noble squares, streets, &c. &c —A
circuit of the town made by the author —Pastry-
cooks —One third of the inhabitants of London
dwell

dwell in cellars —Footways, their conveniency, but why seem to have been made —Walking in the streets, why dangerous.—Cause of there being more cripples in London than in any other city —The English surgeons in general deficient in skill —John Hunter apostrophised—his character —General appearance of London—not a showy capital—houses too little ornamented, and too uniform—built with bricks of a dismal hue—windows resemble holes in walls —Iron rails have a heavy dull effect —The Thames a noble river, but entirely concealed from view —These defects made up by a number of conveniencies, some of which are specified.—The author's wish that this country may experience no revolutionary frenzy

LETTER XIV —Page 194

OF THE ENGLISH STAGE

The author frequently visited the theatres, and why—saw all the principal pieces—Mrs Siddons, the muse of English tragedy—her figure, style of acting, stage requisites, &c —Mr Kemble —Mrs. Pope —Mrs Esten —Mrs Powel —Comic performers of extraordinary excellence are—Miss Farren—Mrs Jordan —The English musical taste advances towards perfection—Storace—Madame Mara —Mrs. Crouch's singing would be admired in Rome, or Naples —Mrs. Bland — Miss De Camp —Incledon —Kelly —Dignum —The author laments the loss of Edwin—Bannister, junior, the actor best pro-

b

mising

mising to fill his characters—his performance of
Scapin and the Apothecary in the Prize —King —
Lewis —Kemble —Strange travesties and grimaces
of Dodd and Suett.—Singularities of the English
stage—actors frequently bowing to the audience—
changing sides with each other—Ohs! and Ahs!
dwelt upon and extended.—Declamation of the Eng-
glish stage.—Accent, pronunciation, action, justly
united, form a perfect declamation, which varies
according to the country.—Shakspeare's plays not
acted as he wrote them—which are his most pathetic tragedies. —Macbeth criticised. — Shakspeare's
comedies not so often acted as his tragedies—yet have
great merit.—Falstaff a most diverting character.—
London wants larger theatres —Jane Shore, Venice
Preserved, the Grecian Daughter, the Gamester
more moving than Shakspeare's tragedies —Apology
for the conduct of the English tragedies —English
comedies licentious—those lately written less faulty
in this respect.—French fashions.—Pads.—Grecian
mode of dress adopted.

LETTER XV —Page 225.

ON THE ENGLISH LANGUAGE.

Different effects of knowledge and ignorance of a language.—The English a language easily acquired,
and why—if learned from books not understood
when spoken—Sheridan sensible of this.—Quotation
to this purpose from the preface of his dictionary.—
The English language copious and rich.—A proposed

posed new edition of Johnson's Dictionary, with more than twenty thousand additional words.—The Hebrew tongue has not more than seven or eight hundred.—The English derived from the Teutonic. —The German a more difficult language.—An English lady's observation on English music, which the author applies to the accent of the language —The English have borrowed a number of words from the French language —*Ennui*, why not naturalized?— The English language compared with English industry.—English poetry admirable —Voltaire's observation on the French language.—Dr Johnson's remarks on Spencer and Dryden, quoted, and applied to the English language and literature.

LETTER XVI —Page 241.

THE DINNER

The author invited to Hammersmith, by the Margravine of Anspach, describes the reception there of the company of Fishmongers, with their ladies, who land from their barge, at the Margrave's villa, on the bank of the Thames—he embarks on board the barge with their Highnesses the Margrave and Margravine —land at London-Bridge, and repair to the company's hall, where they are entertained with a sumptuous dinner and a ball, of which the letter gives a full description.

the mouth and never on the cheek —The author's observation on a compliment made at table peculiar to the English—apologizes for the gaiety of his style and changes the subject —The English fond of their children—are humane—instanced in the regulations of boxing —Combats observed by the mob —They pay great respect to departed friends —Funerals —English character much influenced by the riches and commerce of the nation

LETTER XIX —Page 295.

FONTHILL

The author, under the similitude of a dream, gives the Countess de V——— a description of the magnificent country-seat of William Beckford, Esq in Wiltshire.

He accompanies Mr B to Fonthill—the road described —heaths—Salisbury Down—Stonehenge—the noble house of Fonthill—its delightful gardens—the grotto —the temple of Hercules—temple of the Naiad of the river —Mr B's character—his immense estates —his extraordinary accomplishments and mental endowments —Sends two members to parliament for the borough of H —Shrewd reply of an elector for the borough, to a candidate who was chosen

LET-

LETTER XX.—Page 315.

THE COUNTESS DE v———'s ANSWER TO THE
FOREGOING LETTER,

In return, she relates her dream, in which she thought
the shade of her deceased father appeared to her, and
gave her a relation of the enjoyments and occupations
of departed souls, in the regions of bliss.

ADVER-

ADVERTISEMENT.

THE translation contained in the following sheets constituted the amusement of some anxious hours, during an irksome residence at Bremen, whilst the remains of the late unfortunate British continental army were embarking at Bremerlehe, in the year 1795, on their voyage to England. The original work was then but newly published at Zurich, under the title of *Souvenirs de mes Voyages en Angleterre,* (Recollections of my Journies to England) On my arrival in London, in the following year, finding that a few copies had reached that metropolis, and had been well received; and having further learned that no author by profession had undertaken to translate the work into English, I reviewed my former labours, and being encouraged to commit them to the press, I now, with all becoming deference, submit them to the perusal of the candid English reader.

The author, a Swiss by birth, is named Henry Meister; he resided, for twenty

b 4   years

years before the French revolution, at
Paris, in quality of correspondent and literary agent for the Empress of Russia, the
Duke of Brunswick, and the Margrave of
Anspach, together with other northern
sovereigns; a character in which the great
Voltaire himself appears to have been employed by the princes of the house of Bran-
denburgh, and which, though it does not
entitle the person bearing it, to be enrolled
in the *corps diplomatique*, is yet necessary
to promote the benefit of society; and, if
not so honourable, is, perhaps, a more innocent employ than that of an avowed spy
under the protection of letters of credence,

Mr Meister is now, or was lately, at
Zurich, in Switzerland, and is supported
by a pension allowed him by the Margrave
of Anspach. He is esteemed, by those
who know him best, as a worthy and respectable man, possessing much literary
knowledge, and more taste.

Upon the original work, and my translation, I beg to be allowed to make the
following observations;

I have

I have thought proper to number the letters, which the author has not done; and whereas he judged it only necessary to give a word or two to explain the subject of some of the letters, I have, to all, given a full account of their contents. what I have added, will be known from the author's heads of contents, as they are printed in capitals, and accompany the letters themselves. I may, perhaps, be thought to have too officiously obtruded myself with the notes; my intention, in such of them as remark on the English words he has introduced, has been to assist the reader's judgment on the author's qualification for a critic on the manners and customs of the English nation, from his proficiency in the language of it; for these, as well as for the rest, I hope this general apology will be accepted. As to the author's principles in philosophy and politics, he has given some ideas on them in his own advertisement to this work; and the following list, which I shall take the liberty of giving the reader of his writings, will prove that he must be

an

an author of no small estimation on the continent.

1 *De la Morale Naturelle*, (Of Natural Morality) printed in 1788, in a small volume

2. *Des Premiers Principes du Systéme Social appliqués à la Revolution présente*, (The first Principles of the Social System applied to the present Revolution). The last edition printed at Paris, in 1791.

3 *Conversations Patriotiques*, (Patriotic Dialogues). The last edition at Paris, 1792

4. *Lettres sur l'Imagination*, (Letters on the Imagination), printed at Zurich, 1794 —Besides a great number of articles on philosophy and literary subjects, printed in the foreign journals, or published with other collections.

The author's descriptions are every where elegant and lively; he sees objects in a point of view peculiar to himself; seizes on them with a boldness of observation, and offers them to his correspondent with a correctness of judgment; and this in such a style of animated language, that they are presented before him clearly and discriminately. An author with such powers of wit and depth of thought, writing in a language highly cultivated, graceful

ful and eloquent, is not easily followed; I have taken, therefore, great pains to do him justice in English, and have not always been satisfied with my own diligence; happy, however, if the candid reader shall accept of my exertions with indulgence.

Improprieties and absurdities constantly presented to our view, by becoming familiar, are so far from appearing shocking in our eyes, that we embrace and pursue them with a degree of prejudice and favour, from which we are with difficulty to be withheld. The use, then, that may be made, of a perusal of the accounts which travelling foreigners have given of our country, is, that our eyes may be opened in this respect, and that we may correct such of them as they have impartially pronounced to be deserving correction A further use may even be made of the very mistakes and errors which such authors have fallen into, which is, that we may be thereby induced to make proper allowances in our judgment of the manners and characters of foreign nations, and not give implicit credit

to

to accounts of them written by travellers of our country: and these gentlemen themselves may be thereby induced not to hazard their censures too rashly; or, like our author, and the writers of post-haste observations, run into false representations and erroneous opinions Lastly, The remarks on the English nation, made by a foreigner, may serve an English reader, in some degree, as a description of foreign customs and manners, since it is natural for the writer of one country to make observations upon those of another, which vary in any respect from his own.

THE TRANSLATOR.

THE

THE AUTHOR'S ADVERTISEMENT.

THE former Letters of this collection had appeared in the *Journal des Indépendans*, before they were printed together in a small volume, and published, in 1791, at Paris. Afterwards, M. d'Archenholz translated some of the letters into the German language, and inserted them in his *Minerva*. M. Reichard was pleased to do them still more honour; for he has introduced all of them into his *Olla Podrida*, as the production of an emigrant lady; whom, to save appearances, he has feigned to be assisted by her brother with some observations, which could not so well have been supposed to be made by herself.

The kind reception which the little volume met with at that time, in Paris, had determined me to leave it nearly as it then was. I should certainly have wished to have made it more deserving the attention of my readers, but I feared lest I might render it still worse in striving to make it better. I

con-

considered that if there were any merit at all in these letters it was derived from a faithful and natural representation of the first impressions of my mind; and that if I endeavoured to enlarge my sketches, and give them more strength of colouring I might hazard the loss of whatever was interesting in them.

The letters which follow in succession after the tenth were never before published. They are addressed to different persons, and written at very different periods of time; from these circumstances they may perhaps have the appearance of contradicting the former ten; but this is occasioned by their being composed with the same spirit. Similar objects, viewed and decided upon in a different manner, according as situations have unavoidably varied the lights they were considered in, will, perhaps, have given room for coincidences of a curious nature.

As I have never been connected with any sect or party, why should I become any more the slave of my own opinions; than

than of those of others? I should suppose, that I am for that reason better disposed to submit them fairly to the advancement of my own understanding, and the prudence acquired by time and experience.

After this declaration of my faith, may I not be permitted to hope that aristocrats and democrats, republicans and royalists, will condescend to grant me, if not their esteem at least some small share of toleration?

Frail and blind mortals as we all are, would it not be too much to promise to see things in the same light to morrow, as we suppose we view them in to day? To revere truth whenever she presents herself to my sight, to say just what I think, are all I dare engage myself for; and I have the hardiness to believe my positions are as worthy of consideration and attention, as those of any systematical writer, or the supporter of any party, whoever he may be. The philosopher who differs most from himself is undoubtedly he who will not change his opinions on acquiring better information, or on their uncertainty becoming

coming more apparent. And what new lights are not to be expected at a juncture of time when, from the multiplicity of events, their singularity, and the rapidity with which they succeed each other, days seem to be as years, and years as ages! Of whatever party a good man may happen to be, whether he is led to it by a chain of circumstances, or has espoused it from conviction of mind, he would become wretched indeed, were he to consider himself under an obligation constantly to share in all its mistakes, and to participate in all its crimes.

Such readers as would give themselves the trouble of fully understanding all I have wished to say, are requested to peruse the notes accompanying the text as they proceed; and I further beg leave to add, that I have made in this edition a number of several very necessary observations, by way of annotations to the first ten letters, which were not in any of the former publications of them.

LET-

LETTERS

ON

ENGLAND.

LETTER I.

GENERAL DESCRIPTION OF ENGLAND--- COMPARISON OF THE ENGLISH AND FRENCH CHARACTER.

My dear Friend,

YOU wish me to give you some account of my tour in England, and for my part I am ready enough to satisfy you in this respect, only premising that you are to expect no pompous descriptions, high-flown remarks, or minute observations I have seen a great deal, and considered more; but there is no book written for the use of

B   travellers,

travellers, however futile or trifling, that
will not satisfy your curiosity better than I
shall be able to do with my post-haste com-
ments; for what I shall have to say will be
rather what I have thought than what I
have seen.

When my stomach was relieved from the
anxiety it had felt for ten or twelve hours
during which we were on our passage, the
first objects I viewed struck me with sur-
prize, when I reflected that in so short a
distance as our continent is separated from
this island, they were so very different.
The soil, the air, the stile of building, the
dress and manners of the people are so
much unlike, as to give us room to suppose that a distance of some ages have in-
terposed to disjoin two nations, which now
seem to have a desire to keep up a communication with, and follow the example of
each other.

Whatever may be the future consequences of this desire or imitation, I confess that I had not walked fifty yards on
English ground before I thought I felt sensations

sations of freedom and the dignity of human nature rising in my breast, which I had never experienced before, not even on that day when, following a number of other heroes as curious as myself, I trampled on the ruins of the Bastile.

I am ready to allow that there is no country whatever where Liberty may not erect her standard, but you must permit me at the same time to believe that she will establish herself more readily on the borders of the ocean, or behind inaccessible rocks, than in open plains *.

Protected by the element which surrounds him, the Islander has no other power to dread whilst he has that to support him. The industry which he is obliged to exert in order to secure a subsistence for himself and to procure whatever superfluities he is desirous of, are the most power ful means of his protection, and he finds

---

* It was an observation made to Mr Walpole, that in order to secure the quiet of one half of Europe we should drown the other.

B 2 his

his ships his strongest defence   He is at home when he chuses; he visits his neighbours as he has occasion.   From whence I conclude that Islanders are from their situation forced upon schemes of commerce, to establish liberty, and encourage a sort of egotism   By egotism, I mean a necessity of separating themselves from other nations, and of having no other communication than as ambition, interest, or inclination may prompt.

Of England I have seen only the road from Dover to London, and some few places round that capital; but I was equally surprized every where with a certain air of neatness which I admired on my first landing.   Every part discovers that appearance of security of property, which is no where else to be found   This is what renders this country so agreeable; which in many other respects is deprived by nature of advantages which she has liberally bestowed on its neighbours.

It should seem, that if we understand by liberty what the vulgar in general mean by

the

the word, and those idle notions which some superficial philosophers have affixed to the idea, a foreigner arriving in France would have supposed freedom existed there long before the revolution, even in a greater degree than in England With the English we are not to look for that behaviour without constraint which carries an appearance of ease and satisfaction; whilst the French, covered though they were with rags, preserved a confidence and courage of deportment in every situation. If their chains were heavy they supported them with chearfulness, and they seemed of little inconvenience A Frenchman appeared to act without compulsion or restraint; thoughtless and vain, the contented slave had the air of being more free than the wisest of the earth, and happier than all the kings of the universe

If I may venture to form an opinion at first sight, (and it is often of a nation as of an individual that the best and truest judgment is to be made in that way rather than by long consideration,) the English discover

B 3   to

to outward appearance none of that natural
confidence which renders a man equal to
every occasion that may happen, and which
is often mistaken for freedom, when no
adequate ideas are formed of the liberty
which well regulated societies are capable
of; with him confidence appears to be the
result of time and reflection.

Under the ancient government a Frenchman seemed by his manner of behaviour
to declare to the whole world, " I am
" master of my actions; it is true, my ex-
" istence here is likely to be shortened by
" some unaccountable caprice, but through
" skill and address, and with the assistance
" of honour and courage, I can escape, with
" more or less good fortune from all arbi-
" trary power. The toils which are spread
" to entrap me are of little consequence,
" since some way or other I have wit or
" courage to elude them."

An Englishman seems to declare himself
more distinctly, and with less artful refinement. He is accustomed to submit to a
certain restraint, and he has a veneration

for

foi the restiaint he submits to. This restiaint is the law, he knows what the law
iequires of him, and he knows the piotec-
tion he expects from it in retuin; upon the
secuiity of the law his whole confidence is
founded, and by it all his actions are regulated. He knows he is not to do as he
himself pleases; but well satisfied with
the libeity he enjoys, he is sensible of his
own situation, of the protection he is under,
of the power he has to do what is right,
how he ought to act towaids others, and how
they ought to act towaids him.

I made an observation soon after my
landing in a mattei not indeed of any great
consequence, but which perhaps might on
that account force itself on me the more
strongly. When the men who biought
our things fiom the packet-boat came to
ask a gratuity for their pains, it was not
done with that importunity which is cus-
tomary in Fiance, which though made in
a polite manner is, however, tioublesome:
here it was a matter of account, in which
each article was explained; the payment

of

of which was demanded without incivility, and indeed without any tricks of deceit by which more or less than what was justly due might chance to be obtained In this country every individual from the *lord* to the *coachman* seems to know better than in any other *what is his just due, and what his fare is to be.*

There is as great an inequality of ranks and fortunes in England as in France; but in the former the consequence and importance of a man as a member of society is far more respectable. Individuals of the lower classes are better cloathed, better fed, and better lodged than elsewhere; and often, as far as I could learn, with no better means than the same classes enjoy with us *. Pride and a desire to preserve the public esteem seem to force them upon that atttention to their conduct and outward appearance.

---

* Poor Count D—— observed on his return from London, that the thief went to the gallows better dressed than many of our celebrated criminals He himself was a proof of the justness of this remark.

Amongst

Amongst us the class of beggars as well as
the order of nobility discover an inclination
for shew and expence; for a person may
act the prodigal as well in rags as in the
splendour of a magnificent house, since
management and order are apparent in the
distribution of the smallest produce of labour and industry.

I do not impose upon you when I say
that though the English labourer is better
cloathed, better fed, and better lodged than
the French, he does not work so hard.
You will wonder at this the less, when you
consider that the wages of the former are
higher, and his diet more substantial, consequently that he has greater strength and
activity in the performance of his task, and
as he applies to it with more assiduity he
finds less frequent calls than the French
labourer to make up by extraordinary exertions for the loss of time through holi-
days instituted wantonly, or occasioned by
indolence or debauch

If the labour of the French handicrafts-

man

man appears more diversified, and more
easy and ingenious, these advantages are
more than compensated by an application,
a patience and attention, which the English
workman is remarkable for. You may
judge what wonderful effects talents like
these are capable of producing, by what
they are able to perform in the manufacture of steel: I have seen a plain pair of
scissars sold for an hundred guineas

The road from Dover to London is, you
may well suppose, a considerable one. It
was in the finest season of the year, and in
one of the finest days of that season that I
travelled it, and I overtook no more than
two travellers on foot, and they were foreigners going to work journey-work. I
knew them to be foreigners because they
were singing German songs. However, the
roofs of the carriages are well covered, and
I have seen from twelve to fifteen persons
perched upon the tops of some of these
coaches, and amongst them several women
who

who from their appearance were in good circumstances *

Perhaps

---

* Is there any thing possibly more contradictory to the good sense so conspicuous in the English nation than this absurd custom of riding on the outside of a coach? It would seem as if these people were under the cruel and constant necessity of removing from place to place, and that to do it with more speed and convenience they laid aside all fear of danger It is calculated that every Monday no less than fourteen hundred vehicles set out from London, that is to say, public ones, such as dilligences, coaches, as well mail, hackney, as stage coaches, &c some with four wheels, some with two, three, eight, and ten These with ten wheels are built in the shape of a gondola compleatly covered, and may accommodate from thirty to forty passengers, the wheels are low, and they are drawn at a good pace by four horses The expence of travelling in these public carriages is not great, and not above two pence or three pence a mile, which is about four or six sous of French money The English traveller, whether by land or water, but more particularly on horseback, displays an extraordinary degree of resolution For this reason it is that we see more wooden legs here than in any other country, and that the loss of a limb being so common is less thought of than elsewhere In every great town, and even in the smallest village it is easy to procure a vehicle, and as many horses as you have occasion for, on the shortest notice The letting out to hire post-chaises and post-horses is in the hands of the public at large, and inn-keepers vie with each other

Perhaps I had heard too much said of the pleasure I should receive from the agreeable verdure of England to be struck by it. It is certain I did not receive so much as I expected, and I cannot but think I have seen as fine a verdure in some parts of Switzerland, and even in France, in some spots in Normandy, and the country of Boulogne. What I could not but admire was the inclosures of green hedges kept up in such good order; and the great neatness which appeared in the dwellings of the cottagers with the well furnished shops which were every where to be seen in the smallest villages I was not quite so well pleased with the custom of presenting at every stage glasses of punch and bowls of brandy and water, which circulated from one man's mouth so politely to that of his next neighbour. I did not approve more-

---

in readiness of accommodation You have scarcely settled for the stage you have run, before your baggage is shifted to another chaise, the horses put to, and the postilion ready to drive you on to another.

over

over of the large table-cloth which covered the dining-tables, and were used to wipe your mouth and fingers in the place of napkins: I did not like the linen the better for smelling so strongly of smoak; nor do I relish that heady strong *porter*, nor *small beer* which tastes like a ptisan, nor the rich muddy *port.* However, I make no doubt but I shall soon be reconciled to English cookery; for I know nothing more nourishing, or that I could eat more frequently without being cloyed, than a good beef-steak with potatoes, plumb-pudding, and good Cheshire-cheese, &c.

LETTER

LETTER II.

DESCRIPTION OF LONDON—REVOLUTIONARY ANECDOTES.

WHAT I have so much wished to see, I have now seen—London. You may believe me when I tell you that on my drawing nigh to this noble capital I felt all those lively emotions of joy, satisfaction and repose, which the sight of a great city has ever excited in my breast, after a journey of some days towards, or absence of the same time from it. I know well that a sentiment of this kind has nothing of a romantic or poetical air, nor even rustical, yet I might be under some apprehensions that many people would form but an indifferent opinion of my philosophy, or feelings; but I am incapable of making myself appear better than I am. Whether luckily or unluckily for myself, I find I am rather a cosmopolite than a citizen, and great cities seem to me

the

the general home of all independent and
civilized men, in them, as in a common
center, the talents, arts, industry, science,
and every resource of a country meet, they
are the grand theatres of action and information, from which are derived all the benefits genius and civilization afford the human race. But I must not leave London
before I am well arrived at it

If the most magnificent city is that in
which there are the greatest number of noble
buildings and superb houses, most undoubtedly Paris is far beyond London; but if we
pay more regard to the extent of ground
which a city covers, to the regularity of its
streets, the great number of squares, the appearance of industry and wealth amongst
the inhabitants, it is certain that London is
in these respects much superior to its rival
Except the cathedral of St Paul, which is a
fine and elegant imitation of St Peter's
church at Rome, that remarkable specimen
of gothic architecture at Westminster; Somerset Place, the Bank and the Mansion-
house; I have seen no building worth men-
tioning

tioning   St James's has the appearance of
an old monastery, or rather, if you please,
an old barrack; and the palaces which
have been erected for the Prince of Wales
and Duke of York are models of meanness
and bad taste.   The theatres are indeed
well enough withinside, but without they
look like so many shabby tennis courts.
The Pantheon, Ranelagh, and Vauxhall,
prettily and even richly decorated as they
are, cannot be pointed out as patterns of architecture.

However, having premised thus much
with impartiality, I am scaicely able to describe to you how much I was struck with
this city on the first view of it. The uniformity
of building, which, as it were, set each other
off, seemed to supply every deficiency of
ornament or shew.   The breadth of the
streets, and the singular convenience of the
pavement appropriated for foot passengers,
the variety, the neatness, and the rich shew
made by such numbers of shops of every
kind, formed a spectacle of so delightful and
astonishing an appearance, as to conceive

must

must needs be seen   There are so many things laid open to view, and spread forth with so much art and attention, that till the eye is accustomed to sights so various and brilliant it must needs be weary

You are not ignorant that London alone transacts two thirds of the trade of the three kingdoms; the splendour and activity of its retail trade will not therefore surprise you; but to take a view of the extent and grandeur of the commerce of this first trading nation in the world, you must penetrate the busy throng which constantly blockades the Strand, and proceed, as I have done, till you mix with the crowds which fill up every avenue to the Custom-House; you must next take boat to go down the Thames, and see the bosom of that noble river bearing thousands and thousands of vessels, some sailing up or down, going or coming from every part of the world, and others moored in five or six tiers as closely to each other as it is possible for them to be; you will then confess that you have beheld nothing that can

C   give

give you a stronger idea of the noble and
happy effects of human industry.

I confess that such a view of the glorious
consequences of civilization affect my mind
equally with the striking beauties of una-
dorned nature, and that this sight has filled
me with wonder and admiration. It is impossible to observe the many conveniences
which this noble river affords England without calling to mind the celebrated reply
made by a Lord Mayor of this city to one
of their kings, who, being displeased with
the citizens, had threatened to remove his
court from London; " Your Majesty," said
he, " whilst you deny us the favour of your
" presence, will at least permit us to enjoy
" the advantage of the Thames."

This reply which is as remarkable for
the singularity as the shrewdness of observation contained in it, confirms me in an
opinion which I have ever maintained, that
the happiness and power of a people depend as much on the advantages of their
situation, as the wisdom of their government;

ment; in the same manner as the happiness
and success of an individual depends no less
on his natural disposition, than on the circumstances of his fortune, and the regularity of his conduct.   We must therefore
consider when we admire the excellent
frame of the English constitution, that the
nation does not owe all the benefits it enjoys
to that alone; that much is due to the necessity it is under to extend its commerce;
to the local situation of the island; and *to*
this great river, whose proud waves waft
with every tide the riches of the universe to
the very walls of its capital.

I will add another observation to those
already made, which is, that the advantages
of local situation and the genius of the soil
being most to be depended on, a constitution, in which these points are not attended
to, or, as it may likewise happen, are essen-
tially injured by it, must be the most unfortunate and fatal that can be imagined—
But, since you may be inclined at this instant to attribute this remark to a particular
party-spirit, which cannot be sufficiently

guarded against, I shall not further elucidate this argument.

After viewing all that was to be seen of London by traversing its public walks, its streets, markets, taverns, and coffee-houses, I have not omitted to visit the playhouses, the churches, the prisons, the hospitals, and the two Houses of Lords and Commons; but I shall defer to another opportunity to give you an account of the manner in which I was affected by these different objects.

What I cannot omit observing at this present moment is, the surprise I was under when I considered the quiet and regularity which prevailed amongst such vast crowds, constantly in a state of agitation. During the whole fortnight that I have been in London I have been continually moving about from morning to night in one part or other of this populous city, and in the most frequented parts of it; and yet I have met with fewer disturbances and frays than are to be seen at Paris in one morning: this order and regularity is however preserved by a police of from eight to twelve

hundred

hundred men. There is a great difference
betwixt this number and thirty thousand
national guards with pay and without; but
so it is, that a constable, armed only with
the single staff of his authority, effects more
here in London, than all the crimson en-
signs of our august municipalities are able
to do at this juncture in Paris. What a
length of time is required for the law to
obtain that respect and authority which
is necessary to secure the strength of an
empire!

I saw a boxing-match one day betwixt
two men who fought desperately; one of
them was a servant, the other a labourer;
they were surrounded by a circle of spectators who stood quietly viewing the contest,
and did not offer to part the champions till
one of them acknowledged that he was
conquered. None of our duellists of the
Bois de Boulogne, not even if they had been
legislators, could have discovered more
coolness nor greater conformity to the rules
of single combat, than did these noble com-

C 3   batants

batants with the fist amidst the throng of Pall-Mall.

One of your democratic principles would possibly be much hurt to find such frequent use made in London of the epithet *royal,* which is affixed to all sorts of shops. This reminds me of a story which I learnt at Paris, where this old-fashioned epithet has given place to that of *national .* A man, who exhibited wild beasts on the *Boulevard,* had omitted to write on his show-cloth the *large royal tiger,* and had substituted in its stead these words, " *Here is to be seen the large national tiger.*" I need not tell you that the sign did not remain long with these words; perhaps it might be thought productive of some aristocratic comment; however, the inventor of the alteration could have no other view in it than the pleasure or advantage which he hoped to derive from the compliment, which, in the simplicity of his heart, he thought he had paid the nation.

LETTER

LETTER III.

PLAYHOUSES.—SITTING OF PARLIAMENT.

THE first time that I was at the theatre in the Hay-Market, which during the summer is the principal one in London, my love for my native country was agreeably flattered in observing that most of the ladies who filled the rows in the boxes exactly followed, in their head-dress and other ornaments of their persons, the Paris fashions. As there were amongst them a great number of very pretty women, it took some considerable time of observation and reflection before I perceived that this imitation was not always attended with a good effect; perhaps this remark would not have suggested itself at all but for the presence of two or three Parisian ladies*, who were easily dis-

---

* See Lady C——'s observations upon the author's account of the English ladies in her letter to him.—Translator.

C 4   tinguishable

tinguishable from the rest of the females,
and by whom I was led to compare the co-
p es with the originals*. The piece that
was represented that night was a translation
of *Le Barbier de Séville* (the Spanish Bar-
ber,) the music of Paesiello adapted to the
English words; so that you see I was quite
at home. This piece appeared to me well
acted, as far as I could judge of a dramatic

---

* The English ladies appear to have regular features and
fine white skins, but in general very little animation in their
countenances. As in ancient Greece, if we are to give credit
to M. Paw, so, in my opinion, more handsome men are to
be met with in England than handsome women, especially
from the age of eighteen to twenty I particularly admired
at first the beautiful tresses of the ladies, and was surprised
to find they were all either black or a dark chesnut. I was
told that the colour was settled by the fashion, or, to speak
more plainly, that they wore false hair, such is the present
rage The custom of wearing false hair is not altogether
new in England, for Moryson, who lived about the age of
Shakspear, speaking of the dress of the English ladies of his
time, says, " Gentlewomen virgins wear gowns close to the
" body and aprons of fine linen, and go bareheaded with
" their hair curiously knotted, and raised at the forehead,
" but many, against the cold, as they say, wear caps of hair
" that is not their own."

performance

performance in a language to which I was
but little familiarized, and whose accent
was quite new to my ears; but as to the
music, though it was generally applauded,
it had so singular effect upon me, that so far
from discovering the delicious melody of
the airs of this composer, I could perceive
nothing else but English country dance
tunes varied more or less happily. If our
language is heavy and drawling, and badly
adapted for musical expression, that of our
neighbours is in my opinion still more so;
and do you not find that the articulations
are too rough, too short, and too little ac-
cented? I have seen twelve or fifteen
pieces played whilst I have been in London, and of that number I could find that
more than half of them were either translated or imitated from plays received on our
stage When we consider the two countries in this respect, and in others of far more
consequence, do we not see that these ancient rivals in interest and glory have agreed
to copy from each other? Alas! if to our
misfortune our new constitution bears such

a re.

a resemblance to that of the English nation,
as their fashions do to ours, what are we to
think of such an imitation? Aukward attempts of this kind are not easily amended,
and the slightest error in points of legislation has effects of a very different nature from mistakes in the article of taste and
fashion.

Whilst France seems to slight the advantages annexed to monarchical government,
England seems at this present moment to be
sensible of the influence which this branch
of their constitution has over the strength
and quiet of the state. There is no proof
of affection and respect which was not
shewn the King during the course of his late
indisposition and long convalescence; for
several weeks past that his Majesty has been
perfectly restored to health, the famous mo-
tet of *God save the King* has been constantly
called for in the theatres. I must relate to
you what I was witness to at Sadler's Wells;
after *musick, musick,* had been repeatedly
vociferated in no very melodious accents, I
heard *God save the King* called for in still a
more

more thundering manner; impatient without doubt at such repeated bawling, I distinguished a voice which was heard above the rest, and which, with a peevishness that set all the spectators in a roar of laughter, cried out, *God save the King, God save us all.*

As during the summer season the most celebrated performers of Covent-Garden and Drury-Lane do not condescend to act at the theatre in the Hay-Market there are few tragedies represented there. I have therefore not had the good fortune to see Mrs. Siddons, the Clairon or Dumesnil of the English stage, but I have been much pleased with the performance of Mrs Kemble, Mrs. Brooks, and Mrs Bannister; the first especially appears to be an actress of great simplicity and feeling, and I found a great resemblance in her of Mademoiselle Doligny. Mr. Edwin must certainly be a great proficient in his art, since a great part of his acting being of course unintelligible to a foreigner, I fancied I understood every thing he meant to express; there is certainly something irresistibly comic in the

turn

turn of his features and tone of his voice.
Comparing him with two others whom I
have known famous in that stile of acting,
Préville and Raffanelli, I must give Edwin
the preference, who seems to unite a more
natural gaiety and vacant simplicity to the
niceties of their comic performances. It
may appear singular and well worthy of
remark that at this present moment the
greatest comic genius is not to be found
in France or Italy, but amidst the fogs of
London.

At the representation of such pieces as I
could accompany with the book in my
hand, I lost no part of the plot and design,
nor even the most lively parts of the dialogue; the *Minor*, indeed, and some other
little farces excepted, in which the caricatures were either so local or extravagant that
I could comprehend nothing of the author's
intention; they were, however, to all appearance very diverting, for the audience
laughed greatly at the performance. There
being great licence in the most regular comedies, it may be well supposed that there

is more in these　I enquired under what controul the theatres were, and was informed that the correction of the stage was confided to the Lord Chamberlain, an officer appointed by the King　Do not say a word of this to Messieurs de *** and C** for they will be shocked at it; and think it a proof of their argument that the true principles of liberty are not well understood in England.

London is now in its first enthusiasm on account of the French Revolution, and I have seen the *Taking the Bastile* represented at Sadler's Wells, Astley's, and the Royal Circus. These pantomimes were formed from the famous *Revolutions of Paris* by M. Loustalot, and contain the most shocking and affecting circumstances of that work, collected with great discretion and moderation. You may be sure the iron cage and skeleton within it have not been forgotten, which are dragged out of a dungeon with horrible outcries, and have a wonderful effect To efface the impression made by such melancholy scenes the representation is closed with

with a beautiful decoration representing Britannia seated in a triumphal car, holding transparent portraits of the *King and Queen of Great Britain*, which she offers for the homage of the audience accompanied with musick and singing.

The print-shops are besides full of caricatures relative to the transactions now going on at Paris. In one, Liberty is represented seated on the ruins of the Bastile, and the *grand Monarque* receiving from her hands a crown with these words, which issue from the mouth of the goddess, " This it is not " in the power of time to destroy." In others the allegory is less noble; we see the unhappy prince there swallowing the constitution which is presented in a rude manner by Philip Capet, and the elder Riquetti; being seized with a qualm of the filthiest sort, he is made to say, " Do you suppose " this will go down like the wing of a " chicken?"

The meetings of the House of Commons, at which I have been able to be present, have neither been very full, nor on very

interesting

interesting occasions. There was one matter of importance that I saw concluded,
which was a new tax on tobacco; but the
grand debate happened on the night before,
when I was not in the House, and whilst I
was there there was no debate at all.

I had, however, the good fortune to view
at leisure the person of that virtuous young
man*, who, in the violent age of the passions,
discovers all the calmness and discretion of
maturer years; who, from his first setting
out on his political career, shewed himself
equal to the support of that immense succession of glory which he derived from his
father; who, amidst the most violent strug-
gles for power, obtained the confidence of
all parties, and under the most critical and
trying circumstances attached the nation
more than ever to the throne, stepping forward in defence of royalty, become from
a melancholy calamity a mere shadow,

---

* The original is *le vertueux jeune homme* —Translator.

which

which he effected with a zeal and courage only equal to its success *.

Accustomed as I was to the tumult of our National Assembly, you may judge if I was not surprised to find in the House of Commons such decency, order, and stillness. But what was my astonishment when I saw the speaker open the meeting with a long prayer, which the assembly appeared to attend to with proper respect! But I saw neither archbishop, curate, monk, or vicar. To be sure the people who filled the seats of this assembly are very unlike those who occupy with so much majesty the tribunes of our august Riding-House †;

I did

---

* There is nothing remarkably striking in Mr Pitt's features, they discover, however, a depth of attention, with a great degree of calmness and intrepidity. His carriage and appearance are rather slovenly and careless. The only advantage he seems to derive from his years is that serenity of mind which is the happy concomitant of youth, there is, moreover, at times, a certain vivacity in his looks.

† I ask pardon for this democratic appellation. It has been pretty often proved that this assembly is no other than

an

I did not observe one person who was not properly dressed, which is a proof how great an influence aristocracy has over this nation which calls itself a free people. I was informed that if the auditors became in the least troublesome, a motion from any one of the members was sufficient to cause them to be turned out. The regulations of the House with regard to their own members are equally rigid; should an honourable member by speech or conduct merit the censure of the House, he would be instantly committed under a strong guard to the Tower, and if the offence was thought worthy of it, condemned to ask pardon of the House upon his knees I was shewn a gentleman who some years since underwent such a humiliating sentence for some indiscreet words he had made use of, he had

---

an exercising ground in which our knights of the revolution have displayed their dexterity, as at a tilting-match, and where every feat of skill has been exhibited by Jacobins and demagogues It was there they first gave lessons in the fatal tactics of insurrection, to which they have since become the unfortunate victims

D a ma-a malicious kind of wit; and after he had received the usual reprimand and was risen up, he affected to brush the dirt off his knees, and spoke out loud enough to be heard, " *I never saw so dirty a house in my life.*"

LETTER

LETTER IV

OF THE BRITISH CONSTITUTION—OF POPULAR ELECTIONS

YOU have known for a long time the regard, nay, enthusiasm, which I have ever entertained for the spirit of the British constitution. I see nothing in ancient or modern history comparable to it, in my opinion it is the perfection of political combination; there is to my thinking none, wherein the different powers which form and support society, are blended and balanced in a manner more likely to give strength to the executive branch of the constitution, and secure liberty in its full energy. By a happy mingling of every form of government, the one moderating the other, and all together forming by union the most powerful degree of strength, the same effect is produced as in the human body, in which by an equal mixture of

D 2

tem-

temperaments, sound and perfect health is
produced. I was applauding my invention for this happy allusion, when by ill
luck for my vanity, it came into my mind
that it could be no other than a recollection
from Aristotle, who in his Politics, more
than twenty ages back, has made use of the
same comparison.

Much as I hold in veneration the leading
principles of the British constitution, you
are not to suppose that I am equally an admirer of all its results. Their criminal jurisprudence* was for a long time the only

one

---

* Criminal Jurisprudence still retains much of its ancient barbarity in many respects The indulgence which
this code shews is often as cruel, as its severity is sometimes
shocking The smallest theft is punished with death The
greatest degree of violence may elude the pursuits of justice.
But the wisdom and humanity always to be found with juries render the sensible mind free from apprehension in criminal matters on account of the defects in this dreadful
code. Nothing can be imagined more solemn and affecting
than a sessions at the Old Bailey, the most essential points,
as well as the most trivial, are strictly attended to The
questions put to the criminal by the judge have all the appearance

one in Europe which philosophy and humanity had no occasion to blush at; but it is at present to my mind outdone by that which the Emperor Leopold has established in Tuscany I am not fully master of the subject, not having sufficient acquaintance with the British laws, and cannot therefore

---

pearance of cool and collected justice, which, without partiality, discovers a conscientious sagacity, and an anxious desire of giving innocence every opportunity of working its own deliverance The summing up of the evidence is performed by the judge in a manner which appears to be dictated by wisdom, candour, and humanity, pointing out to the jury the matters on which they are to determine. Should the judge have omitted any part of the evidence, every person in court is at liberty to set him right, but he must do it with that respect and deference which is due to the administrator of the justice of the nation, otherwise the audience would resent it as an insult When the judges come in court they are presented with very large nosegays by women of the lower sort, besides which, the tables at which they sit are covered with flowers and aromatic herbs, as is the bar at which the prisoner is placed Over the bar looking-glasses are hung up, which serve to cast a reflexion on the faces of those under examination, that the workings of the countenance may be visible If no traveller has made this observation before me, as I think there has not, I judge it very necessary not to omit it here

undertake

undertake to point out to you the particular matters wherein they may be said to be defective; but I must insist there must be something wrong in them when they are liable to be evaded by the guilty. When crimes are multiplied, the hope of impunity becomes at once a mischief to society, and affords an example which must be attended with bad consequences to the morals of the people   I know not whether I felt more surprise than indignation when I was informed that there was a man, named Barrington, who had escaped punishment more than twenty times because he was more expert as a lawyer than a thief.   My love of liberty is not blinded to that degree that I would give up the measures so necessary to secure my life and property.   I feel more sensibly the necessity of existing in security, and enjoying in peace the fruits of my industry and labour, than of preserving my independence, which, in a state of society, is no more than an imagination, more or less agreeable, or more or less reasonable.

The municipal laws of England stand, it

should

should seem, more in need of reform than
the criminal, for from all I could observe
or learn, there is no country in Europe
where suits at law may be maintained on
slighter grounds, nor where you are more
certain to be ruined by gaining them. Justice, which being so noble a thing can never
be too dear at any price, is, however, to be
had only at a higher rate in England than in
France, under the old form of government.
The law, which permits you the enjoyment
of your liberty on giving reasonable bail,
was certainly dictated by equity; but it
cannot at the same time be denied that it
confers a monstrous privilege on the rich
man, and is hardly reconcileable to those
principles of equality which the National
Assembly would fain set the rest of mankind a madding about   What appears in
some measure to compensate for this privilege is the power which a man in distress
has of seeking justice *in formâ pauperis*, by
which all the expences fall on the adverse
party, whether the suit is gained or lost.
But this regulation, however, appears to

D 4   encourage

encourage chicanery and every device of
the most cruel injustice.

The decision of matters in dispute by a
jury, or by the country, as it is called, appears to me to be attended with great in-
conveniencies, and perhaps, retains still
something of the brutal ignorance of the
times from which it derives its origin.   I
cannot easily reconcile to myself the idea
of my fortune, my life, or my honour, de-
pending on the whim or obstinacy of one
man, or upon the resolution of his eleven
colleagues to withstand hunger and confinement   I cannot but acknowledge that
it is with extreme diffidence I venture to
condemn an institution of which long experience has shewn the advantages, and
which one of the most enlightened nations upon earth has always venerated and
esteemed.

I shall not attempt to prove to our demagogues that the national representation of
England is as compleat as it ought to be;
it is very certain the English people are not
represented in the two Houses with that exactness

nctness of proportion which our legislators
have considered as so very essential, the
secret of which they suppose they have discovered in the united relations of territory,
population and contribution. Without dis-
puting with them the truth of the data on
which they build their system, I will only
take the liberty of observing that, in my
opinion, the prosperity or freedom of a nation are not matters that depend on the
nicety of calculation. The great inequality
which must always result from the vast di-
versity of disposition, interest, passions, and
particular talents of the different representatives, cannot but destroy that equilibrium
which it appears to be the principal object,
and the whole study of the united efforts
of our sages to preserve. It is impossible
to submit the movement of the grand political machine to so nice and delicate a
trial. An empire containing five and
twenty millions of souls is not to be ana-
lized like a problem in geometry; because
the irresistible influence of prejudices, the
caprices of imagination, and the jarring of
interests

interests of so many various dispositions and
tempers cannot be taken into account in
this analysis, however wisely, however ex-
tensively, however precisely made.   The
springs therefore of a great machine must
not be too refined or complicated, but sure
and simple, and capable of producing the
effects required from it readily and with
ease.   •

Laying these principles aside, I think I
can perceive that the great interests of the
people, the protection of their persons and
property are effectually secured by the formation of the House of Commons in which
rests the power of framing laws relative to
the imposts and duties   Though the privilege of naming these depositaries of their
power of legislation is not so divided that
every individual of the people can be said
to have exerted his right of choice in proportion to the extent of his means, it is nevertheless certain that their election is made
by the people.   Now, it is equally certain,
that a body elected by the people can have
no interest distinct from their electors;
especially

especially when the duration of their office is limited, and when the whole power and consequence of their situation depends on the degree of confidence they obtain from an exertion of their zeal, and the full force of their talents, in the performance of the duties of their charge.

The House of Lords appears to me to be the perpetual existing representation of the wealth and prerogatives of the nation Its power is less active than that of the House of Commons, it is a power of resistance and repulsion, this House being at once the bulwark of the King's prerogative and the freedom of the constitution; in short, it is a power which regulates and confines within proper limits, as it were, by the simple weight of the personal consequence and interest of its members, the other branches of the constitution; and in which the true principles of the strength, the wisdom, and the durability of the British government are to be looked for This branch of the constitution well considered, it will appear, how wisely this considerate nation, after securing
ing

ing its laws and liberties from the dangerous
attacks of royal and ministerial influence,
has guarded against influences equally fatal,
I mean democratical influence, dema-
goguical influence, and an influence which
I shall take the liberty of stiling *populaciar**,
for the word popular has been too much
abused not to require the necessity of coining one less equivocal.

To conclude, supposing the English nation to be sensible of the defects of their
national representation, and how far it is
from being compleat, I can venture to prog-
nosticate that after the violent commotions
which have been experienced in France in
consequence, they will be extremely cau-
tious how they venture upon making the
experiment of reforming abuses, or trying
alterations with a view to improve their
constitution. They will be of the same opinion with the sagacious Israelite†, who, be-

---

* In the original *influence populaciere* —Translator.

† This was M Ephraim of Berlin, who was at Paris in
a diplomatic character from the court of Prussia.

ing

ing roundly asked by one of our Jacobins, whether he did not think that all Europe would imitate the French in their revolution, replied, " I cannot certainly say, but " it appears to me that people in general " never have recourse to strong physic till " they are well assured that they are sick."

One of the means which has preserved the British constitution from too powerful an influence of democratic principles has been, that the greatest part of the elections rest in the hands of the King *. The people keep those only which indispensably belong to them; they chuse their representatives and their chief judges; because being chosen by themselves they cannot refuse to repose in them that confidence which is necessary for the performance of their duties. All other offices and dignities, and nearly every other employment, are at the nomination of the King and his

---

* See the remark upon this, as well as what is said with respect to the office of a Judge being at the choice of the people, in Lady C———'s letter.—Translator

ministers,

ministers, the majesty of the throne being
thereby preserved; and what would a throne
be when stript of its majesty? There is another reason for it, because it would be impossible that the executive power should
have all its necessary vigour and strength if
all its engines were not under its command
and consequently within its choice. And,
lastly, because betwixt the dilemma of court
intrigues and popular ones, it has been
judged safest to run no risk of defending the
constitution against the former. When the
people are left to their own choice they
must of necessity often make many bad
ones, still more that are indifferent; from
this very reason that they are easily misled,
and that they are not likely to be called to
account, and that the bulk of the individuals which compose the mass of this sovereign power have no other consideration
than how they shall sell their votes to the
best advantage. To this it may be added
that the people are most apt to despise those
who are their own creatures, setting up an

idol

idol which they worship this day, and trample under foot the next.

The monarch, surrounded with ministers who are responsible for their conduct, has no interest so great as making a choice justified by success; and, in a free country like England, he has every opportunity of informing himself by public opinion of the real merit of the men he has to chuse? A prudent desire of becoming popular is undoubtedly conducive to the welfare of the people; but when it is carried to too great a length, when it extends to every the minutest detail, when it becomes, as it were, the principal, the only means of arriving at power, it circumscribes great talents within too narrow bounds, and actually reduces a free people to a nation of slaves and sycophants. It is far better to suffer a few courtiers to cringe about the throne, than to see a whole nation debase itself by such vile dispositions. This was exactly the case of old Rome; the clients and slaves of the *Forum* were easily converted into
the

the supple tools of Tiberius and Caligula,
as the transition of our courtiers in becoming the most zealous advocates for the nation was readily effected.   The mask only
is changed, the man is still the same.

LETTER

LETTER V

SUNDAY—THE ENGLISH DELIGHT IN THE COUNTRY—WOMEN.

I NEVER had so good an opportunity of finding out the best manner of paying my devotions to the Supreme Being as on the last Sunday that I staid in London. I began with saying my prayers at the Spanish Ambassador's chapel, I afterwards went to a chapel of Methodists, where I was soon tired with a barren superfluity of common-place morality of the most rigid and scrupulous kind. From thence I went amongst the Quakers, and waited half an hour in silence the motions of the spirit, which condescended on that day to work with a very mean instrument, for I heard only three or four sentences, of little significance, stammered out by a single friend who was moved to open his lips. I concluded my pious expedition by stepping into a church

E

of

of the established religion, where I was
much edified by a discourse full of sound
doctrine, and the sublimest tenets of religion   I was greatly affected by the exem-
plary modesty and piety of the preacher's
deportment, and the respectful silence and
attention of the congregation.   The deliberation with which sermons are delivered
from the pulpit is the more striking and
remarkable, as the pronunciation of common discourse is so very rapid   It should
seem as if the language of the church is
different from that of the stage or conversation.

Sunday in London has more the appearance of that day than it has in Paris; it is a
day set apart from the rest of the week, and
particularly dedicated to divine worship,
to quiet recollection, and rest from all avo-
cation   The common people rise earlier
on Sundays than on working-days, and
after church they either go some distance
out of town, or walk about the skirts of it
It is in the country that the English seek a
retreat from care, or at least have that intention.

tention. The chief display of their wealth,
and their greatest expence are at their
country houses. There they deposit the
most valuable effects which their industry
and the great activity of their commerce
have imported from foreign countries, and
there the productions of every age and climate are to be found. A great part of the
most admired labours of Greece and Italy,
and of Rome, both ancient and modern,
have for a century past been transporting to
this new Carthage, and are actually to be
met with in the villas of this happy Island.
I have had an opportunity of seeing only
a few of these collections, but those few
have delighted me.

It was early in the month of August that
I went to dine with *Mr The***, at his
country house nine miles from London.
I never saw finer fruit than was brought in
with the desert, pine apples, peaches and
grapes, the most delicious that can be ima-

---

* I suppose Mr Thellusson's at Bromley in Kent.—
Translator

E 2　　　　　　gined.

gined. M. de Lauraguais* presumes to say
that he never met with any ripe fruit except
some baked apples, but I can assure you I
never tasted finer fruit at Paris. It is true
that the hot-houses of Mr. The— are
spoken of as the finest in the kingdom.
The stables, at these country seats, are an
object of curiosity. It is no wonder that
the English horses are so beautiful when so
much care is taken of them. Certainly, in
no part of Europe are horses better fed,
better housed, or more attended to And
as to horses of blood upon which a great
value is fixed, it is saying no more than
truth to assert that it takes up the whole
time of a man to look after one of them †.

I do

---

* It is well known that M de Lauraguais was so impertinent as to say, on his return from England, " that he had
" met with nothing *polished* but the steel, nor any *ripe*
" fruit except baked apples '

† The fiction of the Houynhoums is no where so applicable as in England The horses are as numerous as the
human species, they are kept as neat as the men can possibly keep themselves, and, in fact, when one considers the
manner

I do not know whether the English manner of riding is more graceful than the French, but it is certainly lighter, and gives the animal an opportunity of exerting its full powers; and, in reality, I think experience decides in favour of the English practice of riding

In France, when we had nobility of high rank, if any one of them outran his fortune, he went and shut himself up in his country house; in England, when a nobleman has ruined himself he either retires to London, or travels abroad, for a journey into a foreign country is actually a saving of expence, as they reside at their country seats only whilst they are able to live in a style suitable to their birth or title. You may from this be able to judge of the different kind of esteem which is paid to rank in the two nations In the one, the nobility come among their country neighbours

---

manner in which these quadrupeds are attended to, it would seem as if the biped was destined to serve them, rather than they the biped.

to diffuse plenty and happiness; in the other, they go into the provinces only in search of money, which is collected with all the rigour that ruined fortune and the uneasiness of their minds may be supposed to occasion *.

If there is any possible state of happiness existing in this world, it is that which an English family enjoys when assembled

---

* Certain political privileges are attached to the British peerage which no other rank enjoys   The English are, however, very tenacious of distinctions which arise from descent, and the proofs of these are to be traced in a college of Heralds, which has existed since 1340   There are at this juncture many Peers of the realm who, according to this college, are not nobly descended , as it was the case in France at the time when M de Beaufremont observed he was the only gentleman in a company composed of Dukes and Blue Ribbons   The King of Great Britain may create as many Peers as he pleases, but it is not in his power to make a gentleman, nor to give the Peers of his creation the arms of another family   in such a case the Herald's-College would not permit them to make use of such assumed arms   Great respect is paid to coats of arms, and upon the death of a gentleman the family-coat is displayed on the outside of the house in a large black frame during the whole time of mourning.

amongst

amongst their houschold gods in the country; blest with the gifts of nature and fortune, protected by the wisest of constitutions, and the integrity of the public mind,
they are equally secure from the encroach-
ments of an absolute power, and popular in-
surrections, situate in a country which has
received every improvement from industry
and wealth, amidst the most delightful and
romantic prospects, they receive every
mark of respect and esteem, and repose
themselves in the most perfect confidence
and security. Every thing about them
discovers a taste for domestic happiness,
with a relish of the sweets of solitude and
the beauties of nature. You cannot pass
two days in the country of England without discovering that it is the only place in
the world which must have produced the
most interesting stories, and the happiest
families. The female sex are so beautiful,
their reserve so amiable and affecting, their
general deportment so modest, that even
vice cannot withhold its esteem and respect. The youth of both sexes are edu-

E 4   cated

eated together; and the easy familiarity which subsists betwixt both, conciliates the passion of love, awed and subdued by the exactest attention to the laws of decency Compare this picture with the pollution of a great city. In London corruption of manners has fewer charms to adorn it than we have had skill to invent, and consequently its influence is less dangerous and fatal Modest women are therefore in more plenty in England, than in other countries, and for that reason more happy and respected.

I cannot say the same of those women to whom the world has denied the claim of modesty. There are not fewer common women in London than in Paris; and though there are amongst them many who are exceedingly handsome, yet they do not make that figure which courtezans, distinguished for the beauty of their figure and persons, do in France. The only kept women, who live in any degree of elegance at London, are French girls who, having

met

met with then lovers abroad, have followed them hither

As a traveller should see every thing that is to be seen, I did not fail to visit the house in London where the best is to be met with of what may be styled bad company You must not expect from me descriptions which the liveliness of your imagination may dispense with my giving I must, indeed, be another Rousseau to allow my pen to be so licentious I will content myself with remarking that we were much delighted with the serious solemnity of the *waiter* when he enquired what was our pleasure? Your notary, or your confessor, could not look graver, or pronounce with a more solemn voice, *Sir, where would you be buried?* The young beauties to whom he had the goodness to introduce us, had very regular features, fine skins and good complexions, but their constant use of beer, butter, and strong wines, deprived their breath of its proper delicacy; and is besides the cause, as I am informed, that they are not distinguishable for that beauty, which

makes

makes a part of Tasso's description of Ar-
mida, *mamme acerbe e crude*   I do not
think I shall be charged with presumption
when I affirm that M de Caraccioli, the
Neapolitan Ambassador, was in the right
when he maintained, that if the English
women were more cleanly before men,
the French women were so before God.   I
have no doubt there are many exceptions,
and those very amiable ones; but it is possible that in general the morals of the people would reject those refinements of cleanliness, which border upon an affectation
of luxury and softness of manners,   Rousseau said, Sophia is either ignorant of, or des-
pises that excessive cleanliness of the body
which defiles the soul; she is more than
cleanly, she is undefiled   Sophia is in the
right; but Sophia has kept her secret from
all the world.

LETTER

LETTER VI.

PRISONS—HOSPITALS—GREENWICH-HOSPITAL.

WOULD you, my friend, think yourself happy to live in a state of society? In order that you may think so you must visit the shops where rich manufactures are produced; you must go to sea ports like those of London and Amsterdam; you must see the vast number of objects which genius and luxury, the arts and sciences display in great cities   Is your imagination disposed to gloominess? Would you be eloquent? Visit our prisons, our hospitals, you may there consider at leisure human nature in disgrace, the evils, the mischiefs which the fatal ferment of the passions, the poison, more or less active of social institutions, bring upon mankind   But after the first emotions of your indignation or pity, your sagacity will lead you to reflect that society,

so far from nurturing these seeds of corruption which our nature cannot but produce,
is the very means of checking their growth,
or pruning their luxuriance   If the vices,
which society is charged with producing,
had not first existed, society itself had never
been formed   Without a natural inequality, how should social inequality ever
have been established? Without the necessity resulting from property, how should
laws ever have been thought of to protect
it?   Our legislators, you see, are like Sosia,
they came before they arrived.

I was conducted the other day to see
Newgate: What a horrid sight! As we
crossed the court yard where the prisoners
assemble who are allowed that indulgence,
I was attacked as by a swarm of harpies,
and had no means of escaping but to throw
a handful of halfpence amongst them, for
which they scrambled with all the fury of
a parcel of wild beasts who have been kept
without food for a number of days*.
Whilst

* Newgate is the most perfect piece of architecture of
any public building in London, it is peculiarly adapted, by
its

Whilst I was set upon in this manner by these, others, who were shut up, stretched forth

---

its style of building, for the purpose to which it is designed, and strikes the spectator with a degree of horror The few ornaments which decorate it are all emblems of the use the edifice is appropriated to, they are awful and without embellishment Before one of the doors the scaffold is erected for public executions, and remains no longer there than is necessary I had resolution enough to attend an execution Figure to yourself a kind of theatre encompassed with a double chain and hung with black The dismal sound of a bell declares the moment when the victims of justice are brought forth I shall never forget the horrid preparation The executioner was a full quarter of an hour in adjusting the rope about the necks of two wretched malefactors who had been convicted of robbery They both cast their eyes around with the cord fixed about their necks, one while looking at the Ordinary, then at the spectators, and then at the beam to which the rope was fastened, with a calmness which might astonish a mind more courageous than mine After some exhortations, which the silence that prevailed amongst the spectators gave every one an opportunity of hearing, they sung a psalm or hymn The executioner then pulled a cap over their heads which concealed their faces entirely from the view of the spectators In this situation the Ordinary continued some time addressing them, and at length descended slowly from the stage to rejoin the sheriffs seated below At that instant the platform, on which the criminals stood, dropped like a

piece

forth their hands through the iron bars, venting the most horrible cries. I was accompanied by a turnkey, who kept them in order as a huntsman does a pack of beagles; one word, or even a look from him, was sufficient to stop their clamour. He pointed out to me the window of the room in which Lord George Gordon was

---

piece of theatrical machinery, and left them suspended from the beam to which the ropes were fixed Their death was consequently as sudden as possible , besides which, the friends of the malefactors are commonly near, and if any sign of agony is observed they pull them by the legs to terminate their misery the more certainly and speedily. Shocked as I was with this awful spectacle, I was not less so when I observed a number of men and women carried to the scaffold to be stroked by the hands, still quivering in the agony of death, of the suspended criminals, under the notion that such an application will be of efficacy in working a cure for several complaints , amongst the rest I remarked a young woman, with an appearance of beauty, all pale and trembling, in the arms of the executioner, who submitted to have her bosom uncovered, in the presence of thousands of spectators, and the dead man's hand placed upon it.— Cruel, incomprehensible superstition ' thus to outrage the good sense, the decency, and decorum of an enlightened people '

confined

confined for a libel against the Queen of
France When will our laws have vigour
and activity sufficient to do the same for
our C——, our M——, our R——, &c
&c? You may well suppose that I could
not long support the impressions which the
sight of this dismal mansion made upon my
mind; but in going out I met with a subject to excite my pity and astonishment
I was shewn, in a court surrounded with a
wall which seemed to reach the skies, a
young Jewess, of a most interesting appearance; and I was told that she had solicited
to be shut up in this doleful situation, that
she might afford comfort to her father, who
was to suffer for coining, during the short
time he had to live. He had confessed the
crime, and, sensible of his approaching fate,
his whole thoughts centered in his daughter, whose countenance and manner discovered the tenderest attachment of a piety
truly filial, mixt with a degree of grief and
resolution

From the few observations I was capable
of making, and from all I have been able to
learn,

learn, I do not find that there is more humanity, or that there are fewer abuses and irregularities in the English prisons than in those of France. I am of opinion that, during M. Necker's administration, through the generous compassion and noble bounty of his worthy and amiable lady, the prisons of the Hôtel de la Force were more healthy, and kept in better order than this gaol of Newgate I say nothing of the King's-Bench, which has more the appearance of an asylum than a place of confinement; such as was of late years the Temple at Paris. The walls of the King's-Bench include a considerable space of ground with entire streets of very comfortable dwellings. M. d'Archenholz, in his journey to England, has given a very advantageous account of this place, to which I must refer you. Many a philosopher, nay, perhaps, a monarch, would think himself happy to enjoy the quiet of such a retreat. After having made a sacrifice of liberty, it is impossible to find a place where there is more security and independence What I am

dis-

dissatisfied with is, that, in making choice
of this place of confinement in preference
to any other, it is absolutely necessary to
pay down a sum of money; five or six guineas, as I believe. To continue there any
length of time it is something more. Money! for ever money! How is it that in
every circumstance of life, whether fortunate, or unfortunate, this talisman, money,
still preserves such a powerful and settled
influence?

Of all the establishments intended to al-
leviate the evils of society, to succour indi-
gence, to comfort decrepitude, and console
unfortunate virtue, and which at the same
time confer an honour on the victims of
courage and love of their country, I know
not one in the whole world comparable to
the hospital for worn-out and disabled sea-
men at Greenwich It is situated on the
banks of the Thames, at the distance of six
miles from London, and is actually the
finest palace in England It is composed
of two buildings separated from each other
by a grand esplanade, in the middle of

F which

which is erected the statue of George the
second   These two buildings exactly cor-
respond to each other and terminate each
with a dome of noble and elegant architecture; the front towards the Thames is
composed of a double row of Corinthian
pillars, in couples, which support the pedi-
ment.   The more we admire the magnificence and elegant taste discovered in these
two edifices, the more we are hurt at not
finding some building to connect the two
extremities.   It is true the perspective is
closed with the governor's house, but this
erection, which stands unconnected with
any other building, is so mean in itself, that
it rather disfigures than fills up the space.

But what an assemblage of grandeur,
elegance and beauty of design, to make up
for this omission! The terrace is one of
the happiest situations, in point of prospect,
perhaps in the whole world.   The pen-
sioners from it may see daily passing along
the noble river which washes its side, vessels returning from every part of the globe
whither their former fortunes may have led
them;

them; and thus amidst the happy quiet of their retreat, they may renew the recollection of past enjoyments or dangers, the whole adventures of their lives, their early voyages and their last labours. Behind this splendid house of refuge is a beautiful park, well furnished with trees, from certain elevations in which a very extensive prospect presents itself, including a remarkable fine view of the city of London.

The greatest order and regularity is observed in this superb hospital. The exactest discipline, and the utmost cleanliness and neatness is every where to be met with; nothing is wanting that can tend to the production of repose and conservation of health, the very paintings of the hall and chapel serve to recal to its inhabitants ideas of calamity and conquest, with reliance on the goodness of Providence, and gratitude for the bounty and protection of their country

How little do they know of the movements of the human heart, and of the main springs of those virtues necessary to society,

F 2

who

who are not sensible, that if private charity should be studiously concealed to become more meritorious, it is far otherwise with the charity of a nation! Public charities cannot display too much pomp and show; they should appear striking to the imagination. The rewards of a nation, nay, its very alms should be consecrated by monuments of magnificence; those who partake of public charity, so far from being humbled by the bounty, should esteem it a mark of honour to be admitted to receive it.

I had written the last words, when I received the strictures which follow in the next letter. It is an English Peeress, not more distinguished for her birth than her wit and genius, who has condescended to take me to task for some observations contained in my former letters. I mean to avail myself with all gratitude and humility of her Ladyship's remarks. I send you the letter in question, and when I resume the pen it shall be to answer it.

It was a pity I was forced to break off so, for I had it in my mind to have said a deal

more

more to you of the famous Tower of London and its noble Arsenal; of the collection of pictures in the possession of Mr. West, and Sir Joshua Reynolds; of the splendid Gallery of Shakespeare, of the immortal works of our friend Fuseli, the Dante and Shakespeare of painting.

Lettre de * Milady C***** à l'Auteur

DES ABUS DE LA CONSTITUTION AN-
GLOISE—DIFFICULTÉ DE PEINDRE LES
ANGLOIS TELS QU'ILS SONT.

Mon cher Monsieur,

VOTRE feuille littéraire de Mars contient
quelque chose sur quoi il faut que je vous
parle.   Ce sont vos lettres sur l'Angleterre.
Dans une des premières, vous aviez vu tout
ce qui regardoit le costume et le maintien
de nos fèmmes aux spectacles, dans un jour

---

* Any Note from the Translator may here, perhaps,
be thought unnecessary, as no reader of taste can be at a
loss to supply the letters wanting to make out this name,
who has ever heard (and what reader of taste has not
heard?) of the elegant manners and polished wit of the
amiable and accomplished Lady Craven

The Translator is well informed that the Author, to
whom this Letter is addressed, maintained a correspondence with Lady C , during her stay in the dominions of
the Margrave of Anspach, but had no permission from her
Ladyship to print this letter

si absolument contraire à la vérité, que j'avois répondu en plaisantant ; mais j'ai brûlé ce que j'ai écrit, ne croyant point qu'il importoit à la dignité de ma Nation que vous nous trouviez *gauches* avec *les cheveux teints,* et loin de cette grâce qui vous a fait distinguer deux ou trois Françoises au beau milieu de nous. Mais comme tout ce que vous direz sur la législation sera lu avec avidité par les philosophes et les patriotes du monde, et qu'on y croira aussi pieusement que les Péthion, les Robespierre, etc. croient qu'ils font une Constitution, je vous dirai, en amie, que vous vous trompez quand vous dites *qu'on a laissé la plus grande partie des élections entre les mains du Monarque* Le Roi peut créer un Pair quand il lui plaît, et par conséquent donner le droit à quelqu'un qu'il croit *à lui,* de voter dans la Chambre-Haute ; mais ce qui est *élection,* le Roi n'y peut rien.

N'allez pas imaginer que je me fâcherois quand vous diriez à l'Europe entière ce qui s'est glissé d'abus dans notre belle Constitution ; mais vous ne connoissez encore que

F 4   trop

trop superficiellement et les beautés et les défauts, le mal ou le bien de mon pays. Vous n'y avez été que trois semaines; vous vous êtes étonné, mais pas assez instruit, pour être en état de le peindre, si ce n'est que vous ne puissiez vous croire assez amusant ou assez instructif pour intéresser vos lecteurs, même en dissertant sur le pays de la Lune, ou sur tel autre monde que vous n'aurez vu qu'au travers d'un télescope. & ce télescope, c'est une manière de voir Françoise, parce que vous avez resté si long-temps à Paris, qu'en dépit de votre esprit, de votre douceur et de votre bonté naturelles, vous systématisez et vous raisonnez à la Françoise.

Vous ne savez peut-être pas qu'un des grand vices de notre Chambre-Basse, c'est qu'il y a des membres qui tiennent leurs siéges par voix de boroughs et non de province; que tous ces boroughs plus ou moins corruptibles se vendent et s'achètent; qu'il y en a dont les voix électives ne montent pas à vingt, à dix Jugez quelle prédominance de pouvoir pour un Ministre, quand, par de

l'arl'argent seul, il peut commander le nombre prépondérant des voix pour faire passer les actes qu'il veut.

Dans la Chambre-Haute aussi, c'est un très-grand abus de ne pas avoir limité le nombre des Pairs. Ce Roi-ci en a tant faits qu'on souhaiteroit presque d'oublier ce nom de Milord auquel on a attaché tant de gens bas et peu faits pour le porter *

Le peuple ne choisit point ses Juges. Si vous croyez qu'être membre de Parlement donne quelque chose à faire ou à dire sur la législation du pays, vous vous trompez. le membre de Parlement (des Communes) choisi par une Province, est

---

* L'influence royale ou ministérielle de la Chambre des Communes ne pourroit elle pas être également circonscrite par une loi qui ne permettroit au Monarque de dissoudre le Parlement qu'après une époque fixe, comme celle de deux ou trois ans, qui défendroit au moins d en proroger la durée au-delà de quatre ou cinq années ? Car, quel autre moyen de prévenir le despotisme ou l'anarchie d'une grande assemblée, que le droit de la dissoudre à volonté, droit contenu lui-même ensuite par la nécessité d'en convoquer immédiatement une autre ?

obligé

obligé de porter les pétitions de cette Province pour les *bills* qu'elle veut faire passer; mais ces bills ne regardent pas les lois du pays, ni les litiges de la Province. C'est, par exemple, les habitans qui veulent faire un canal de communication entre deux rivières, faire clorre des pâturages publics appelés chez nous *common land*, détourner un grand chemin pour l'abréger, créer un nouvel échange de terres respectives, toutes choses qui ne peuvent se faire sans la sanction d'un bill. Il est obligé de présenter les pétitions ou requêtes: pétition pour ôter tel ou tel impôt, pétition pour élever un hôpital; enfin, tout œuvre qui regarde le grand bien public de cette Province; mais les procès ou les disputes se vident devant un autre tribunal, quand les Juges nommés font leur *circuit* dans la Province.

Croyez-moi, mon cher M......, avant d'achever vos lettres sur l'Angleterre, allez-y encore; allez surtout à la campagne; là, vous nous verrez dans toute notre sublimité: là, vous verrez que chaque maison, chaque

par-

particulier a sa manière d'être à soi. En gros,
nous ne pouvons être peints, mais en détail,
variés à l'infini. Chaque Anglois a son âme ou
ses manières d'une originalité à lui; chacun
s'occupe ou s'amuse selon sa manière de
sentir ou de voir, et c'est de ces contrastes
bizarres que l'Angleterre, pour tout être
raisonnable, est le pays le plus amusant que
j'aie encore vu Je n'ai jamais lu une bon-
ne et impartiale description de mon pays;
les étrangers le louent ou le méprisent trop.
Rarement un étranger voit beaucoup de ce
qui est véritablement grand ou méritoire
chez nous, pour des raisons qu'il ne me
plaît pas de détailler par lettres; presque
tout ce qui fait vraiment la gloire de notre
nation est à l'écart, est retiré chez soi;
comment un étranger peut-il chercher cela
dans son foyer? L'étranger est promené dans
la dissipation de Londres, et là (à ce qu'on
m'écrit), il ne manque à nos femmes que de
déraisonner sur les mots *Constitution et Pa-
triotisme,* pour que ce Londres ressemble
infiniment à Paris.

Mais allez-y encore une fois, allez-y,
connoissez à fond la Cité, vous y trouverez

des hommes qui réunissent en eux tout
l'esprit sobre de notre commerce actif et
l'esprit patriotique des anciens Romains,
avant qu'ils fussent noyés dans le luxe.

Fuyez la Cour, à moins que cela ne vous
amuse un moment de voir *the King in his
state coach going down to the House of Peers*,
et le groupe d'enfans royaux dans le palais.
Allez à la campagne, dans notre Derbyshire,
dans nos villes de Manchester, de Birming-
ham, de Liverpool; allez dans nos ports,
dans nos chantiers; dînez chez nos fermiers,
voyez mes sœurs, mes cousines, les premières
femmes de l'Angleterre faire six ou huit
milles à pied, toutes seules, aux environs de
leurs châteaux, et sans se faire reconnoître,
soulager la misère ou l'infortune de tout ce
qui les environne, et n'offrant que pour des
instans au public leur faste, parce qu'elles
croient qu'elles le doivent à leurs noms.
Vous trouverez surtout des écoles de cha-
rité, des hôpitaux fondés par ces femmes.
Vous verrez des mères de famille dans
toutes les classes, qui frémiroient d'horreur
si elles devoient mettre leurs enfans en pension

sion chez une nourrice, coutume *Françoise*
dans toutes les classes, dont j'ai gémi mille
fois. Ah! peut-être que le temps n'est pas
bien éloigné quand je pourrai vous dire :
-venez voir l'Angleterre de chez moi.

A propos, j'y vais le mois prochain, le
* * * m'accompagne. Vous avez le temps
de m'écrire avant mon départ, laissez-moi
savoir si vous pouvez lire ce griffonnage, et
si vous trouvez bon la franchise de votre
amie

E. C.

*.., ce 13 *Avril,* 1791

Translation of Lady C*****'s *Letter to the
Author.*

OF THE DEFECTS OF THE BRITISH CON-
STITUTION——DIFFICULTY OF CHARAC-
TERIZING THE ENGLISH NATION.

My dear Sir,

YOUR literary journal for the month of
March contains matter upon which I must
have

have something to say to you.   I mean your *Letters on England*.   In one of the first you appear to have seen every thing respecting the dress and behaviour of our ladies at the theatre in a light so very opposite to the truth that I had written to you on the subject in a strain of pleasantry; but I have since burnt the letter, because I considered it of no consequence to the honour of my country that you found us *awkward*, and that we were wearing *dyed heads of hair*, or that we did not carry ourselves in so graceful a manner as did two or three French women, whom you distinguished in the midst of us by their peculiar gracefulness. But as what you have said on our legislature may be eagerly read by the present modish philosophers and patriots, and may be credited by them, as implicitly, as Pethion, Robespierre, &c. believe they are framing a constitution, I must tell you, as a friend, that you are mistaken when you say *the greatest part of the elections rest in the hands of the King*.   The King may create a Peer

when-

whenever he pleases, and consequently
confer a right of voting in the Upper House
to any one who is attached to him, but the
King can do nothing in an election.

Do not suppose that I should be mortified if you were to tell all Europe that
abuses have crept into our noble constitution; but you have as yet too slight an acquaintance with the beauties and defects,
the good and evil, of my country. You
were in England only three weeks; you
were astonished with what you saw; you
were not sufficiently acquainted with the
country to describe it, unless you supposed
you could amuse and instruct your readers
by giving them a description of the world
in the moon, or any other world you have
only seen through a telescope, and that a
telescope after the French fashion: for you
have lived so long in Paris that, notwithstanding your wit, your good humour and
your urbanity, you reason, and you form
systems entirely in the French manner

You do not, perhaps, know, that one of
the

the greatest defects of our Lower House is, that there are members belonging to it chosen by boroughs, and not by the country at large; that all these boroughs are more or less venal, and consequently are corrupted; and that there are some of them which consist of no more than from twenty to ten voters. You may judge what weight of influence is thereby thrown into the hands of a minister, when he can by dint of money alone command a majority of voices to carry any measure he thinks necessary.

In the Upper House there is another very great defect, which is, that the number of Peers is unlimited*. His present Majesty has

---

* I know not whether this and the following note are Lady C——'s or the author's [Translator] It was debated in 1718 "The Earl of Sunderland," says Johnson, in his life of Addison, "proposed an Act called the Peerage ' Bill, by which the number of Peers should be fixed and " the King restrained from any new creation of nobility, " unless when an old family should be extinct To this the " Lords

has created so many that it is to be wished the appellation of my Lord were disused, because it has been given to so many low people who are but little entitled to such distinction *.

The judges are not chosen by the people. If you suppose that being a member of

---

" Lords would naturally agree, and the King who was yet
" little acquainted with his own prerogative, and, as it is now
" well known, almost indifferent to the possession of the
" crown, had been persuaded to consent   The only diffi-
" culty was found among the Commons, who were not
" likely to approve the perpetual exclusion of themselves
" and their posterity.   The tendency of the Bill, as Steele
" observed in a letter to the Earl of Oxford, was to intro-
" duce an aristocracy, for a majority in the House of Lords,
" so limited, would have been despotic and irresistible."

* Might not the royal or ministerial influence over the House of Commons be equally curbed by a law, which should allow the King only to dissolve the parliament at the end of a certain time, say, two or three years, and to prevent its duration for a longer time than four or five ? For what other means is there to oppose the despotism or anarchy of a great assembly but the power of dissolving it at pleasure, a power which is defeated by the necessity of immediately after calling another ?

par-

parliament confers a power of saying or
doing any thing with respect to the administration of justice in my country, you are
mistaken; the member of parliament (a
commoner) chosen for a county is obliged
to carry in petitions from that county for
bills to be passed, but these bills do not relate to the laws of the land, or suits at law
within the county   For example, they
are either bills for a canal to join two rivers;
to enclose public pastures called by us *common land*; to alter the high road in order
to shorten it; to make an exchange of lands,
or some other matter which the inhabitants
of the county are desirous of doing, and
which may require the sanction of a bill.
The member is obliged to present all re-
quests or petitions, petitions to repeal such
and such duties; petitions to build an hospital, in short, every work which has relation to the public good of his county; but
as to suits at law, or matters in dispute, they
are carried before another court, when the
judges appointed for the purpose go into the
country on their *circuit*

Take

Take my advice, my dear Mr ****, and before you finish your *Letters on England*, go there once more, and be sure, go into the country, for you will there behold us in perfection; you will there see that every family and every individual of it has something peculiar We are not to be described in a mass, but by an infinite variety of minute particulars. Every Englishman has a character and sentiments peculiar to himself, there is no individual but employs himself and spends his time in a way agreeable to his own views and sentiments; and it is by reason of these striking contrasts that England is, to every thinking being, the most amusing country I have ever seen I have never yet read any impartial or good account of my own country; foreigners either censure us too much, or are over lavish of their praise It is seldom that a foreigner sees much of what is truly great or praiseworthy amongst us, and that for reasons which I do not chuse to explain in a letter, almost all that in reality re-

G 2

dounds

dounds to the nation's glory is concealed
and hid from him; how then is he to come
at this knowledge, shut up in his lodgings?
A foreigner is conducted amidst the bustle
and confusion of London, and there, (as I
am informed,) that our city may be as like
Paris as possible, are to be found some of
our women who can chatter nonsense about
patriotism and the constitution.

But go there once more; go, and make
yourself thoroughly acquainted with the
city; you will there find men in whom are
united all the solid sense of an active commerce, and the virtuous patriotism of the
ancient Romans before they were immersed
in luxury.

Avoid the Court, unless you chuse to di-
vert yourself for a moment to see *the King,
in his state coach, going down to the House
of Peers,* or the groupe of royal children at
the palace.   Go into the country, into Derbyshire; to our towns of Manchester, Bir-
mingham and Liverpool; see our harbours,
our dock-yards; dine with our farmers;

visit

visit my sisters and my cousins, and behold the first women in England walking on foot six or eight miles round their country houses, and observe them, without declaring who they are, succouring the distressed and unfortunate every where about them, and only at short intervals exhibiting to the eyes of the public that degree of splendour which they judge due to their rank and name. You will find these ladies have, moreover, established hospitals, and founded charity schools. You will find in every station of life mothers of families who would shrink with horror at the thought of putting a child from them to nurse: a *French* custom with people of every degree, which I have been shocked at a thousand times. Ah! perhaps the time is not far distant when I can say to you, come, and see England with me!

Now, to let you into a secret, I am going there next month, and the *** goes along with me. You have time to write to me before I set off, and pray let me know if

you

you can read this scrawl, and whether you
approve of the liberty taken by your friend.

E. C

T   , *Apr.l* 13, 1791.

The *Author's Answer to Lady C*****'s Letter.*

YOUR Ladyship desires to know whether
I approve of the liberty you have taken—
Can you doubt it? I should have been content to have written the greatest nonsense
in the world if it had been attended with
no worse consequence than bringing upon
myself such gentle, mild and edifying cor
rection. However, indifferent as may be
the opinion, my Lady, which you have
conceived from my *Letters on England* of
my manner of seeing and judging of it, I
flatter myself you cannot suppose that I entertained so ridiculous an idea as undertaking the description of a country I had
scarcely seen I did but endeavour to supply the deficiency of materials which the
present barren state of our literature had

occa-

occasioned. I wished only to preserve the recollection of my first conceptions, my early astonishment, and my first feelings; no more If I have been sometimes right in my suggestions; and if now and then I have amused my readers, I congratulate myself to have done no worse.

Having thus candidly acknowledged my faults, my overhaste, and my mistakes, allow me, my Lady, to complain in my turn of the small injustice done me by your accusing me of having said the English ladies were *awkward* I am not conscious of this crime I said no more than that the manner in which they imitated our French fashions was not always happy, and this is, in my opinion, a very different matter To be sincere, I certainly think that there is a degree of gracefulness observable in the French ladies; and, in this respect, I believe there are not wanting English gentlemen who are of the same opinion. Were I to draw the picture of Lady C*****, in any country of Europe, I think, that after I mentioned her original

and

and natural vein of wit, and the sprightly and ingenious turn which so particularly marks her conversation, I should observe, that she possesses the shape and beauty of her country-women; but, in place of saying she has all their grace and attractions, I should, to make myself better understood, remark, that she joins to her other accomplishments all the grace and vivacity of a French lady; and if she was displeased with what I had said, I should have begged to be excused for any prejudices which a residence of twenty years in Paris may have occasioned.

I have expressed myself very ill if I led my readers to believe that I imputed to the King of England any other influence over the elections of the House of Commons than what arose from ministerial corruption; I meant no more than to follow De Lolme and Blackstone in saying, that it had been thought proper to leave to the King the disposal of the greater part of the places, the honours and dignities, civil as well as ecclesiastic; and I commended this power which

which the constitution had conferred on
the royal prerogative as very proper for
maintaining its weight and dignity   We
think, however, very differently of this matter in France, for it has been very seriously
debated whether the King should not be
deprived of the power of naming his ministers.

As for the real defects in the constitution
of your government, it is impossible, my
Lady, to have pointed them out with more
skill and judgment than you have done,
and I perfectly agree with you in opinion;
so much so, that were I to continue my ·
Letters I should this instant beg permission
to make use of yours.   In the mean time,
I shall be very careful that our pretended
patriots are not made acquainted with this
article; it would be giving them too great
a satisfaction—for they are not skilful ar-
chitects enough to know that a few defects
in a great edifice may be amended without
pulling down the whole fabric to its very
foundations

My short journey to England has left me
mole

more to regret than remember. What
would it have been had I had the advantage of your eyes to view the land with,
surrounded as you are with every thing
that can make you value a country which
ought to be as proud of you, as you can be
of it?

LETTER

LETTER VII.

OF SHAKSPEARE.

WE are not now to enquire whether Shakspeare is really entitled to the reputation his works have enjoyed for two centuries, and were the question still open for discussion, it could not be in France, from a plain translation, that his cause could be adjudged. Fame may be usurped for a while without any just title, but a character which has withstood all that time could do to oppose it, that has increased in proportion as the nation has advanced in knowledge and improvement, must be supported by the most incontrovertible proofs, and the plays of Shakspeare could not be at this day the pride and admiration of his countrymen, did they not abound with those sublime beauties which are applauded in every age

Would there be more justice in attempting
ing

ing to discuss the superiority which the English lay claim to for their stage? France undoubtedly will not allow it. But can she be a judge in her own cause? Were she to refer the matter to the tribunal of the different nations of Europe, there is every reason to suppose that Spain and Germany would decide it against us. We might comfort ourselves with the prospect of obtaining our suit in Italy, and especially in Ancient Greece. But would not decisions, so contradictory, declare at the same time a spirit of partiality in the people who made them?

Were it possible to divest ourselves of partiality, and national prejudices, we might say—To judge whether Shakspeare, Corneille or Racine, were the writer of the most merit, we should first examine from whence each of them began his literary career; and we might, perhaps, then perceive, after mature consideration, that the distance from any certain point to the highest degree of perfection which art can attain to, is in reality greater than that of
the

the first commencement of the art from that to which it had arrived at their setting out We should likewise consider the aids and assistance each of them received in his progress; and it might then, perhaps, be discovered that this assistance, and those aids, which seemed favourable to genius, might check his flight, and by preventing him from falling into certain errors, might abate a part of his energy and powers. The man of genius who addresses a nation in a state of rudeness and barbarity, commands and directs them in a manner, and moulds them agreeable to his taste and inclinations. When a people begin to emerge into rule and order, the manners, the customs, the prejudices of such a people, are so many restraints which the man of genius is obliged to respect, and necessarily render his progress less daring and more confined

The critic who should impartially draw a comparison betwixt the theatrical productions of the two nations, would, I think, find that Shakspeare's plots are more various and extensive than those of Corneille

or

or Racine, which have a noble simplicity,
regularity and unity, so much wanting in
the other; but at the same time he would
allow that the plots of the first, notwithstanding their confusion, have the greatest
theatrical effect, and interest the spectator
the most.   Can this be denied when Voltaire has himself affirmed it?   " These
" plays of his," says he of Shakspeare,
" though unnatural and absurd, become
" powerfully interesting.   I have seen his
" Cæsar, and I own that when in the first
" scene I heard the tribune reproach the
" people with their ingratitude to Pompey,
" and their attachment for Pompey's van-
" quisher, Cæsar, I became interested, and
" moved with the representation. Whenever
" afterwards a conspirator came upon the
" stage, my curiosity was excited, and in spite
" of many ridiculous absurdities, the piece
" irresistibly commanded my attention "
And in another place he says, " Of all the
" writers of tragedies, Shakspeare is the only
" one who has not written scenes purely of
" conversation; every one of his scenes ex-
                                    " hibits

" hibits something new, and, in reality, you
" are affected by what is doing on the stage
" in spite of a want of regularity and de-
" corum."

Whilst we acknowledge that the plays
of Shakspeare, viewed in the whole, or in
part, abound in more original and bolder
strokes, we cannot refuse to allow that the
best pieces of the French stage are more
finished, and better conducted. if our tragic poets are to be charged with having departed from the truth of nature for the sake
of adorning her, are not the English dramatic authors reproachable with having altogether lost sight of her, and taking the liberty to aggravate her features? If the style
of our dramatic pieces is often cold and
monotonous, is not that of the English tragedy often loaded with bombastic and
overcharged expressions, and is there not
a want of that preservation of character
which good taste requires? Undoubtedly
it is very absurd to produce servants on the
stage haranguing in the language of heroes;
but it is much absurder to bring on a hero
speaking

speaking like a common fellow. There is certainly a difference betwixt a king and confident, and the manner which marks this difference ought to be striking; it is, however, neither natural or probable, that they should talk a language specifically different, because those who are near the person of their master will converse in a style nearly resembling his. But it is to be observed that in every art nothing can be perfect without harmony. In a piece of painting, if the figures and colours are diversified, we say it is a grand picture; but should these colours not be mixed and united by an agreeable and happy correspondence; if their want of union causes a discordance of the different parts, there will be nothing striking, nothing in the whole, taken together, which shall give satisfaction. The work will interest the common beholder, and will call forth his wonder and astonishment, but the enlightened artist will find something still wanting.

If I were permitted to represent, by comparison the different ideas I entertain of

Shakspeare

Shakspeare and Racine, I should say, that Shakspeare appears to me as a colossal statue, whose-large proportions strike me with awe and wonder, but whose rude execution in some parts, and amazing labour and perfections in others, excite my applause and astonishment; whilst Racine reminds me of a figure like the Belvedere Apollo, which conveys a notion of perfection beyond any thing to be found in nature; and which, notwithstanding the languor I feel in viewing the exquisite finishing of particular parts, delights me with the grandeur, elegance and correctness of its character.

The great mischief which a translation of Shakspeare may occasion in France, will be, if our young men of genius should be tempted to neglect the models which it would be least dangerous for them to imitate, in order to make a vain trial of a style which would neither suit the manners or disposition of the nation It is certainly easier to violate the rules of art than to follow them. Without a doubt it is no diffi-

cult

cult matter to bring together a mass of action, and mingle events of the grotesque
and, terrific kinds; to change the scene
from a tavern to the field of battle, from a
burying-ground to a palace. It is still less
difficult to paint nature as she presents herself to our sight than with discernment suc-
cessfully to cull such beauties as shall discover a refined and discriminating taste.
In a word, it is much easier to disfigure
nature than to ornament her; and if it is
easy to discover the blemishes which de-
form the best productions of Shakspeare, it
is not less so to imitate his defects. But
what other author is endowed with so pro-
digious a genius as, with a disdain of all
rules, by the mere powers of his imagination, to pass current every kind of absurdity and improbability? Who, except himself, can ever hope to throw on designs, of
the greatest size and extent, a light of so
extraordinary a kind as shall render every
part equally clear and luminous? Who,
besides him, can hope to interest the audi-

tor

tor so forcibly, that though he diverts his
attention at pleasure, he can revive his feelings in full strength whenever he chuses?
What writer has so deeply searched into the
inmost recesses and concealments of the
human mind? His works plainly discover
how little he was acquainted with the an-
cients; had he been familiar with the models of antiquity, the arrangement and conduct of his pieces might have been better;
but even had he studied ancient authors
with the diligence the great masters of our
stage have done, or had even been cotem-
porary with the heroes he has drawn, he
could not have represented them in truer
characters, or with more fidelity and exactness. His Julius Cæsar has as much of
Plutarch, as Racine's Britannicus has of
Tacitus; and if he was not acquainted with
history better than others, he must be allowed to have had a lucky guess, and at
least to have hit off characters better than
others knew how

It will ever be a dangerous attempt to
H 2 trans-

transfer the beauties of the stage of any
nation whatever into a foreign language
and for the entertainment of foreigners;
and the undertaking will be more or less so,
as there is more or less difference betwixt
the two countries; and I see a very great
one betwext the French of the age of Corneille and Racine, and the English in the
time of Shakspeare. I do not know if any
very great change in manners has been
wrought since that time, but I see plainly
the design of the English stage has been
very different from ours; theirs has been to
excite the strongest emotions, ours to stir in
a gentle manner our natural feelings, theirs
has been employed to strengthen the manners and character of the people; ours to
reduce and soften them; the one presup-
poses a sluggishness of constitution which
requires stimulatives of the most violent
kind, the other a disposition to receive with
the greatest ease every impression from without, a sympathy of soul ever ready to imitate whatever strikes it with a degree of
force

force*. If this disparity is as great as it appears to us, what possibility is there that the stage of one nation shall be relished by the other? I will say still further, representations of a shocking and frightful kind, may be exhibited to the one people without any danger, but could not be shown to the other without great risk of producing effects very different from the moral intention of the scene

But the observation we have now ventured upon making does not disincline us from thinking but that an ingenious dramatist might derive hints from the English theatre with which he might improve ours. Voltaire has given him an example, and such as might serve for a pattern

---

* Another difference not less striking betwixt the English and French theatres is, that the spectators are sent in pursuit of the events in the one, whilst the events are pursuing the spectators in the other, which is neither more natural or reasonable

LETTER

LETTER VIII.

OPINION OF THE ENGLISH NATION ON ROUSSEAU'S SOCIAL CONTRACT.

YOU are surprized, Sir, that John James Rousseau's *Social Contract* should not have been better received in England. I wonder at it the less, now that that the grand political experiment has been made in France for the happiness or misery of the race of mankind. In a country which has shown us the first example of the advantages and happy consequences of a representative government, can it be expected that a work should be valued, wherein the author maintains that the people cease to be free when they have delegated their power? Considered as a production of genius, the English have found it too dull and abstracted; as a sytematical work, too deep and obscure; dangerous and difficult in its application. In reality, the notions of an original com-

pact,

pact, of the general will and the sovereignty of the people, though sublime and just in appearance, may lead to dangerous errors and abuses For my part, I have been ever of opinion, that Rousseau, with a mind full of headstrong prejudices, had no other end in view when he composed this work, than to show, that, in a civilized state, there was no hope of happiness or quiet

It appears to me that the citizen of Geneva, as well as other political writers who have had recourse, as he has done, to the first origin of society, have forgot that there has never existed a society for any length of time, which has not placed itself under the protection of paternal authority, or some other government, more or less equitable, more or less necessary, or more or less just Where there is no subordination, there is no order; where no governors exist, there can be no governed, no political state, nor even what can be styled the outline of society There must be some form of government long before a settled constitution

Our

Our theories of constitutions are perhaps in
the strictest sense no other than modern notions. Proprietors existed before there were
laws for the protection of property. Property existed of various kinds, and various
sorts of privileges before there was any law
of coercion or security. In a word, nature,
necessity, chance, circumstances had created a social union before men ever formed
a design of constituting themselves into any
society, the farthest even from perfection.

You will not conclude, I certainly suppose, from what I have here said, that the
notions of absolute authority and society
are inseparable, and that despotism is the
first, most ancient and most natural of all
governments. No, you must be too well
acquainted with my love of liberty and my
regard for the dignity of human nature.
But what evidently results in my way of
thinking from the facts I have just stated,
and what I look upon as fully proved from
the ancient monuments of history, as well
as from the ordinary course of human institutions, is, that, previous to the primitive
com-

compact of the citizen of Geneva and his school, there existed certain rights which it became indispensably necessary to reconcile, as being principles of order, justice, and prescription antecedent to any authority the most legitimate, and which ought to prevail over that of the people, as well as that of the monarch. Without doubt the moral, as well as physical world, had an existence before philosophers had ever thought of their sublime theories for its frame and constitution.

The people, as well as monarchs, have it in their power only to exercise a limited authority, whether by an acknowledged and settled right, or by the fixed and eternal laws of reason and justice. A people who should desire to extend the exercise of their power beyond these limits would be in a state of insurrection against themselves; to violate the right to which consent has been once given is to become an usurper; to renounce the principles of reason and justice is to be guilty of self-destruction,

and

and to commit the most atrocious of sui-
cides.

When a people are considered as to their
composition, they will be found to be a
multitude made up of men more or less influenced by their passions, more or less endowed with reason, and more or less ignorant   Considered in a political point of
view, a people will be found a collective
body whose duration depends upon the
union of interests from whence it derives all
its strength, all its rights, and its very existence.   This union, whether voluntary or
obligatory, whether received by descent, or
newly established, has always been antecedent to the political existence of every
people whose history has reached our
times.   In one instance it has been the father of a family and his progeny; in another, a chieftain and his band of warriors;
in a third, a conqueror with the companions of his victory, and the people brought
under their yoke.

This union of interests and power, whether good or bad, whether silently or
openly

openly submitted to, is the first seeds and principle of the natural organization of a political body, and without these seeds and principle, which circumstances only have occasioned, have fostered and protected till arrived at full maturity of growth, this political body could never have had existence. It is not then by a determinate act of the general will that any body of people have been the cause of their political existence, no more than the moral and physical existence of any one of us depends upon his individual will to start into being The deductions to be made from this principle, or rather this fact, appear to me to be of the greatest consequence.

There has always been a primary material in nature, to the modifications of which the genius or power of legislation has been obliged to submit the force of its systems, and the caprice of its fancies and calculations At the very periods when this power appeared the most absolutely to exercise its privileges, there have existed obligations it was under the necessity of observing, and

bounds

bounds beyond which it could not go.
For there is no moral power existing in
heaven or upon earth but is under the
equally irresistible influence of justice and
necessity.

Is it not discovering an ignorance of
mankind, and of the passions to which men
are subject, to suppose that the general will,
of even a small body of people, can possibly be declared with that order, coolness
and precision, which every discussion,
every consultation, must require which has
relation to the exercise of so important, so
sacred a duty, as the framing a law? However august may be the composition of the
representatives of a people, who can thoroughly persuade himself that the general
will of this people, the will of all, can ever
be fully represented by them; that is to
say, with such perfect exactness, that just
equality, as not to render the actual right
of this general will, or the particular will
of each, at once totally vain and illusory?

But I will suppose, if you please, every
obstacle removed, those which appertain

to

to the most perfect democracy, as well as
to a representative government of the best
possible organization   In either case, will
the pretended sovereignty of the people
or their representatives confine themselves
to the present generation, to those men
who exercise it at the present time? Will
the rights of generations which have existed, the rights of generations yet to come
into existence, be considered as nothing,
though undoubtedly appertaining to the
same people? Alas! what then becomes
of the actual power of this sovereignty
which it has not been thought too dear to
purchase with the purest blood, and with
all the crimes and misfortunes which can
afflict human nature! What becomes of
the power obtained at so high a purchase?
It is the fleeting shadow of a moment, a
torrent which in its destructive course
sweeps all before it, and which, owing
to its own violence, is lost and appears no
more.

Immense as may be the extent of the
rights of a people assembled for the pur-

pose of exercising them, should they be suffered to make a trial, though at their own risk, of the daring experiment pointed out by the fable of the phœnix, who, setting fire to her nest, submits to be consumed with it, in the idle hope of reviving from the ashes?

Every power which ceases to be just, which does not respect the limits fixed at once for withholding and preserving its force, cannot but destroy itself ere long In a monarchy or republic no barrier can be leaped over or thrown down with impunity. Can respect be shown where none has been paid? The generation yet to come will avenge itself of that which is past. Destruction provokes destruction. The actual tutelary genius of the fate of empires, as of individuals, is a spirit of moderation and protection.

It will be objected, without doubt, that to hold in such great respect ancient rights, obsolete principles and old customs, will render all perfection and improvement in the situation of society impossible.- Undoubt-

doubtedly it would if this respect was carried to too great a length, and if it was
mingled with a superstitious kind of pu-
sillanimity, but there is a very great difference betwixt such a degree of respect,
and the haughty disdain of every thing
held sacred in former times

The result of my opinion is, or rather
it is what we have been taught from wo-
ful experience, that there is no sovereign
power which is not bound within the
limits of an interest for its own preservation; that the nature and happiness of
man have required that our duties should
take place of our rights; that no generation can consider itself independent of
all other generations, past, or to come,
that if we expect our children should regard us, we must show a regard for our
fathers; that it is progressively, and by de-
grees that good, however apparent, is to
be brought about; and that to render it
of duration we should know how to connect by the most skilful and happy relation the present, with the past and future

LETTER

LETTER IX.

MORE OF OLD FASHIONED POLITICS, BE-
ING A CONTINUATION OF THE FOREGO-
ING LETTER.

WE agree in opinion; for in our hearts
we are all wishing for more power; that is
to say, we want to be rich, to hold employments, to increase our influence, and we
cry aloud for liberty; that is to say, for independence, for impunity, for respect to
our slightest wants, and to our smallest desires.   And are we not in the right? Of all
our natural pleasures is not liberty the sweet-
est, and power the most active?

But liberty is not to be altogether expected in a state of society; for so far is society from giving us more liberty than sava-
ges enjoy, that it but too plainly appears
society deprives us of it ever more or less,
because we are necessarily placed by it in
a dependance on some law or compact. In
my

my opinion we are exposed to the greatest absurdities and errors whilst we persist in deceiving ourselves with regard to this leading principle*.

All that can reasonably be expected from a well-organized society, is, first, the faculty of freely exercising with the utmost confidence and security the several means which we derive from nature for procuring our own happiness without injury to that of others; and, secondly, to extend those means in proportion as the progress of the social system towards perfection is capable of doing it. Every society which does not procure us advantages of this kind makes us but a bad return for our venture in it, as it takes from us more than it gives. It has a right to abridge us of our own liberty; but on this condition that it protects us from that

---

* Aristotle observes, that if we give the popular part of a state too large a share of liberty, we weaken the government, and if we grant too little, we reduce it to an oligarchy

of others, and this can only be effected by good laws

To be free in a state of society is, then, to be governed by laws to which we have submitted ourselves; or more properly, to which we have found it reasonable to submit ourselves: but to have submitted ourselves voluntarily, for example, to a revolutionary government is not in my opinion to become more free.

If we are to depend upon the laws only, it is necessary that those laws should have more strength not only than every individual, but even than the whole body itself, and every association of men capable of conspiring against our happiness, or against that portion of liberty which we reserved to ourselves when we submitted to those laws: and herein it is exactly that the whole difficulty lies

Law is no more than a moral force, and liable to be opposed by a number of other forces, physical as well as moral. The wisest law is, perhaps, no more than an

hu-

human institution, physical force, as well
as the passions which set it in motion, is,
at least, more certainly of divine original.
Whence, then, is the law to derive that superiority of force which is requisite to withstand the opposition—the passions of all?
A law which should be framed with such a
profundity of wisdom, and endued with so
miraculous a charm as to subdue those passions, and that force, would be destructive
of the ends and advantage of society, since
it is in those very passions, and force, that
in the mosst intimate manner consist those
ends, and that advantage. The law, then,
should have force sufficient to restrain them
within proper bounds, but should not have
so much as to destroy them

In every kind of social system, the actual
power of the law can depend only on the
successful use which is made of this moral,
and physical force, with which it is to combat, or rather the influence of which it is to
direct   The law must, therefore, draw
round itself a sufficient strength of this moral, and physical force, to protect itself from

attacks

attacks when most to be feared, and to reduce all opposition where most dangerous.

It would seem at first as if the only necessary measure to attain this end should be
to engage in its defence the most certain
influence of the majority; and this measure
is without doubt the first and principal, but
it is not altogether sufficient for the purpose* There are interests which are ap-

---

* We must not omit to remark here that the real interest of the great bulk of the people does not so much consist in the more or less perfect and accurate distribution of
the powers of the body politic, as in proper establishments
for education so judiciously adapted as to answer their purposes, a religion possessing a proper degree of influence;
laws, plain and simple, tribunals, obtaining and meriting
the confidence of the people, in which justice shall be ad-
ministered at a small expence, and with equal equity and
celerity, a vigilant administration, favourable in its principles to the improvement of agriculture and commerce,
with financial regulations, which at the same time that
they secure government in the most perfect prosperity,
afford every necessary help and support to all branches of
industry As some duties are prejudicial, others at the
same time are productive, and forward the assiduous efforts
of ingenuity and labour England and Holland afford
numerous instances of this sort

parent,

parent, interests which are momentaneous, interests entirely personal, which have more power, a spring of action far more violent than the general interest of all, however evident it may be.

There are passions whose influence, under certain relations, more or less frequent, or more or less dangerous, will always prove superior to the general interest. I shall only name those which are the oftenest in opposition with the maintenance of social order, I mean the passion of acquiring wealth, the love of independence, and the ambition of power and honours.

The seeds of all these passions are sown in the human breast, but it is in proportion to the progress of a state of civilization that they acquire activity, strength, and growth. It is necessary, therefore, that these passions should be restrained and kept within bounds by the force of law. But would not the surest means of conferring on it so necessary a force be to make these passions dependant on, or rather give them an interest in the law which is intended for their

I 3   restraint?

restraint? But what other means so likely
to attain this end as to leave, at the disposal
of the law, all that can conciliate these passions from expectation, and all that can
awe them by fear? Thus the passion for acquiring wealth would find the most certain protection for its industry and property behind the shield of the law, as well
as the most certain punishment for any improper means used in the pursuit. With
this shield, likewise, a laudable ambition
might set out on its surest and most brilliant
career, certain, at the same time, of being
checked with infamy in its course, if it
dared to exceed certain bounds.

If the law could subsist of itself, every difficulty in legislation would be easily got
over. But the nature of things requires
that the execution of laws should be intrusted to men liable to errors, and ruled by
their passions; sometimes to assemblies of
the people, sometimes to counsels, and at
other times to single and unconnected persons. Under every form of government
which can be devised there is danger in
giving

giving those, to whom the execution of the
laws is confided, either too little or too
much power If too little power be given,
the laws become feeble and impotent; on
the contrary, too much power will render
the depositaries of the law arbitrary and
severe

If there existed a class of men in society,
who from their station and pursuits should
of necessity have obtained an ascendant
over the public opinion, an ascendant the
more to be dreaded, as it is less dependant
on the constant springs of the social order,
does there not appear an extreme danger
in confiding to it the guardianship, and execution of the laws?

If there existed a class of men in society,
who have the means of greater physical
force than any other class, and are more in
the habit of using them, whether for or
against the general interest, does there not
appear an extreme danger in confiding to
it the execution and guardianship of the
laws?

Surely, neither the army, nor the clergy,

I 4   neither

neither Jesuits, nor Jacobins, should be intrusted with it; because, by adding the authority of the law to the physical powers
which the nature of things has given to one
of these bodies, or to the moral powers
which in like manner is possessed by the
other, there would undoubtedly be room to
apprehend that a power might be formed
so absolute as to be dreaded   And there
would be reason sufficient for such apprehensions, for every excess of power infallibly produces anarchy or despotism, and
oftentimes both the one and the other   All
excess of power becomes oppressive whether proceeding from a feudal, a popular,
or a divine original; and though it should
not prove unjust it might nevertheless be
looked upon with disgust, and thereby become odious and hurtful.

Enlightened with the experience of these
truths, how is it that we do not see that the
powers of society are to be dreaded when
intrusted to a people at large, since it joins
the greatest moral with the greatest natural
force, the force of numbers, and of every

passion

passion which may agitate the minds of a multitude, collected together by chance? If there was no other objection to a pure democracy than this, I think it would be sufficient to reject it as the most absurd, and monstrous form of government that can be thought of.

Why has a monarchy been so long preferred to every other form of government, notwithstanding its defects? Is it only for this reason that there is no other political system whose springs are so simple, and whose action is so quick? And is it not, moreover, perceptible, that there is no other wherein the power of the law assumes at once an appearance more awful, with a force less unsettled, or less to be dreaded; or wherein this power leaves the individual more at his liberty, at the same time giving him full quiet and security?

All the power of a monarch can be no other than artificial; I mean with a people having, I do not say a constitution, but only customs and laws. He constantly discovers the natural weakness of his power, he con-

continually sees the bounds within which he is confined, and which nothing tempts him to exceed. What does he not possess which can be desirable by man? But what avails his private will so long as it wants the support of the love and good opinion of his subjects? Cicero has said, he cannot govern entirely by it, yet he cannot reign without it. However powerful the monarchy may be, the monarch is always weak enough when left to himself.

I grant that more wisdom, moderation, and œconomy may be found in a well formed representative government. But is it easy to guard against the inconveniences which are the consequence of popular elections? Is it easy to endow it with those principles of stability, without which, neither power or happiness, or even real liberty can exist? And, further, is it easy to give this form of government a sufficient share of those passions, which it is impossible to divest it of, to counteract them, and prevent its working its own downfal and corruption by their means?

As

As all the declamations made by our philosophers, and all the sarcasms they have thrown out against hereditary honours and privileges, apply themselves with equal justice to hereditary property, it is scarcely worth while to reply to them until they are candid enough to confess whether the severity of the great principles of their system necessarily lead to a community of possessions. In the mean time I cannot but see in the succession of privileges, as in that of property, not only one of the most powerful inducements to modern industry, but the surest, and most natural foundation for preserving the duration of every kind of society.

That I may not repeat what I have said elsewhere, I shall confine myself to a single remark. The administration of government is either an easy task, or it is a difficult one, it is so easy, say some of the partisans for democracy, that every man is equally qualified for it. Then why should not the privileged classes of men be equally so? But if it be a task of a difficult nature,

nature, as there is reason to believe it is, why should not a preference be given to men who from a proper education, and studies conducive to this end, may be presumed to be properly qualified? The numbers that may be profitably employed in guiding the springs of the political machine, had need be very few, in comparison with the number of men, which the good and prosperity of the state, and their own private advantage necessarily invite by so many motives to cultivate the arts and sciences, agriculture, manufactures and commerce. It is therefore a point of morality, as well as political maxim, to reduce the one class and increase the other

What government has existed for any length of time, whether monarchical or aristocratic, in which men of superior abilities have not risen to the first offices, however obscure, or mean, their birth or fortune? Moreover, is it at all necessary at this time, that a man of extraordinary talents should be a great officer or minister to become useful to his country? Are there not a thoua thousand other ways in which he may display his ingenuity, and discover his merit? By what fatality does it happen that the people who are so jealous of the privilege of chusing their leaders, or representatives, generally make so imprudent a choice? by what further fatality does it come about that the objects of their choice, even when prudently chosen, become so easily hateful to them?

Power, under whatever name it is defined, or into whatever hands it is surrendered, is always a species of idol; and mankind soon become weary of worshipping the idol they have themselves set up

A power of short continuance is more restless and suspicious than one that is firmly established, it is more liable to be puffed up with pride on account of its accession of grandeur, it is rarely to be restrained by the notion of responsibility, which its pride flatters it with an easy means of eluding; without being iniquitous, its conduct carries an appearance of violence, and inflexflexibility, which becomes odious and disgustful.

Long habits of power, and the quiet enjoyment of an acknowledged superiority. inspire more confidence, more frankness, and more generosity.

The world had been disturbed so long, and in so many different ways with the vices and abuses attached to the influence of wealth, that it had entirely forgotten, in a manner, the vices and abuses attached to the influence of poverty Is no one yet cured of this error, by remarking the use which has been made of the power which weak or evil minded people have thrown into the hands of the latter? And does not the experiment which has been made clearly prove, that a man is not more humane, or a better citizen because he is poor, or that a rich man is rendered by his possessions more cruel, or a greater knave? It is owing to the passions of mankind that the world is disturbed; and the more you divide the administration of the public

force,

force, the more you are in danger of linking the evil disposed, the wilful, and the arbitrary, together

If for a century past we have enjoyed more repose than the history of the most brilliant epochas of civilization has been able to produce an example of, we owe it less to the wisdom of our governments, than to the general spirit of moderation arising from the conflict, or rather from the balance of different systems, which seemed to exercise nearly the same empire over the different nations of Europe, and in a manner checked and controuled each other; the religious systems by philosophical opinions; the system of military authority by that of morality and the laws; the commercial system by the respectable remains of the feudal, and the prejudices of chivalry.

These different systems formed so many barriers to oppose anarchy and despotism; they prevailed the rather because they were not the work of men but produced by time and chance.

LETTER

LETTER X.

WHAT A TRAVELLER OUGHT TO BE.

IF it be so difficult a matter to delineate the true character of an individual, how can we presume to undertake that of a whole nation?

I will confess, that of these two problems I know not which is most difficult to solve, though I may hazard, in saying so, the necessity of maintaining a paradox. There are such fine shades, so delicately peculiar to individuals, that it may require more judgment to discriminate them, than perhaps to discover what the inhabitants of the same climate have in common with their neighbours, or wherein they differ from them. It is more easy to mark a character which frequently occurs than one that is singular in its kind.

The character of an individual is only discovered by actions which are varying

every

every moment, and which are frequently concealed behind the veil of mystery. The general character of a people is open to our view, it is shown in objects ever present to our sight; we may learn it from their language, their form of government, their customs, and their manners It cost Tacitus, perhaps, less trouble to describe the Germans, the Britons, and the Jews, than to paint in proper colours the mind of Tiberius, and the imbecility of Burrhus

Why is it, then, that we find so little truth and justice in the accounts of our travellers? It is because the greatest part of them have not sufficient philosophy or intelligence to comprehend the objects with which they undertake to make us acquainted, another reason is, that there are many of them whose enquiries are made under the influence of party-spirit, and a system which permits them only to see so much as makes for their particular purpose; and a third reason is, because they prefer amusing their readers to informing them rightly, and because they seldom give time

K   suffi-

sufficient to accomplish the work they have undertaken.

Should a person be a stranger in a country, or a native, to be able to give the best account of it?

On first thoughts, it seems as if the person born on the spot, if equal in other respects, should be possessed of better means of knowing the character of his countrymen than a foreigner. Are there not however many points of view on which the foreigner will look with more advantage? To make a proper observation we must be equally aware of the false lights held out on a first-sight prospect, as of habits of frequent contemplation with the same prejudices We pass slightly over such objects as often present themselves, and we behold with too great a degree of astonishment those which are perfectly new. In the first case our remarks are in danger of appearing trite and common, in the second we run a risk of being seduced by a false appearance of the marvellous. In my opinion, therefore, a traveller should mark

down

down every thing according as objects first strike him, but hazard an account of nothing until he has made himself thoroughly acquainted with the language of the country he is remarking upon, its religion, its political constitution, and its particular customs and manners

What renders the knowledge of the different nations of Europe so difficult in our times, is, because we may make nearly the same observation of the various inhabitants of it, as has been frequently made of the people of the same country, that there is a confusion of resemblance amongst them. Manners, politics, and philosophy, have made nearly the same progress in every state of Europe, and each has a like system. The prevailing attention to increasing the size of their capitals, the taste for travelling and literature, and more especially the spirit of commerce, have made the several nations of Europe, as it were, one people. Herodotus would in this part of the world, and in our age, find fewer characters and

K 2

in

in less variety than in the very limited space
to which his history is confined.

However we may suppose that the circumstances which have brought so many
nations into contact may have altered their
original characters, we are certainly deceived if we give a general credit to such
an opinion; their characters are not changed
except in a few features; and, if obscured
by their exterior, they are hard to be discovered, they nevertheless exist.   The
greater the extent of society the more a man
becomes altered, but he cannot altogether
change his nature. If, like Proteus, he varies into a thousand shapes, the eye of genius is able to catch him in his true one.
Italy, notwithstanding all the various revolutions she has undergone during the barbarous ages, and beneath the grievous yoke
of religious despotism, during the long
wars of France and the Empire. yet, did
not Italy, for a long time, maintain that independence and ambition which rendered
her so glorious during the happy time of
the republic?

I think

I think I observed a remarkable difference betwixt the manner in which ancient
and modern nations are to be studied A
great means of knowing the Greeks and
Romans, and the ancient inhabitants of
Gaul and Germany, is to become acquainted with their laws, religion and customs; but to judge of us by the same means,
at this time, would be forming a false esti-
mate We are estranged from our religion,
our laws, and our customs; our manners
and our philosophy have greatly weakened
the influence which they ought to have
over our sentiments and ideas; and a truer
judgment might be made of us from the
spirit of our theatrical entertainments, the
style of our romances, and the taste of our
witticisms than from our jurisprudence,
our worship, or the principles of our government

We have one while endeavoured to imitate in our literature the Spanish writers,
another time the Italian; another time the
English; and they have all imitated us in
their turn; yet, are not these imitations to

be

be discovered by some striking resemblance? Does not the Spanish author essen-
tially discover the sprightly turn which the
warmth of his climate, and the austerity of
public manners produce? Does not the
Italian display the fine feelings of a brilliant
and voluptuous imagination? Is not the
English writer discoverable by the prevailing character of melancholy, which, brood-
ing in solitude, disposes the mind to deep
and solid meditation? And what particularly distinguishes our authors, is it not that
easy manner which the habits of society,
and a peculiar taste for it, give us?

To determine whether the same may be
said of us twenty years hence, we must
know whether our new constitution will
alter our character, or whether our character will alter the constitution.

LETTER

LETTER XI

OF THE ENGLISH CLIMATE——PRESENT STATE OF ENGLAND WITH RESPECT TO THE FRENCH REVOLUTION.

HERE am I, my dear friend, for the second time in England, and you very naturally require of me information as to my second thoughts, whether they are different from those of 1789*. Confess now, have you not a secret wish to mortify the good opinion I entertain of myself by making

---

* As prefaces to books are not perused by every class of readers, the Translator thinks it not impertinent to say in a note what he intended to have said in his *Advertisement* that the author made a second journey to England in 1792 It may likewise be not altogether unworthy of observation that the author has prefixed to the title page of his second volume the following lines from Thomson

Happy Britannia! where the Queen of Arts
Inspiring vigour, Liberty abroad
Walks, unconfin'd, even to thy farthest cots,
And scatters plenty with unsparing hand

K 4   me

me confesss how much I was out in my conception of things on my first journey? That would be no very difficult matter to accomplish, for you know I should not be much concerned about it   There are certain principles of conduct, and some modes of thinking to which I find myself unalterably fixed; but as to my opinions they are mistresses, to which, notwithstanding the violent attachment which you have formerly known me entertain for them, I am not, at this present time, more constant than you yourself have heretofore been. They are changeable, and we too must change with them; but there is no reason why we should not retain a declared passion for them so long as they are amiable; or, at least, whilst they appear so to us. To be candid and ingenuous is highly necessary; and with such a temper of mind, nothing, (whenever that plainly appears,) can give offence, or be thought unpardonable. How many have discovered the same thing in their profound theories and doughty systems, as M. de B*** did all of a sudden

with

with regard to his mistress! With all your
good sense, said one of his friends to him,
how is it that you have not found out, that
the woman you are so enamoured of, is a
monstrous fool? *I thought so myself this
morning*

Agreeable to this little introduction you
will very likely expect to find some considerable variations in this letter from those I
formerly wrote to you. I shall leave you
to judge of them. I will only promise for
myself the utmost sincerity and openness;
your discernment and your friendship assure me every indulgence on your part.

I know well, that your great philosophers and your great legislators have endeavoured to make us believe, that nations
as well as men, are born equal, and that
the difference betwixt a people of one nation and another, is wholly to be accounted
for from the influence more or less apparent of education and government. I do
not pretend to oppose these gentlemen in
their designs or projects; they may, however, possibly find, one day, their principles

ples brought to the test by all the exceptions, all the singularities, all the licence
of nature, in that full force of unconquera-
ble power, with which they have often appeared to me   In the new order of things
I cannot help thinking I perceive those
vast effects that the physical formation of
our organs, the quality of the viands we
are fed with, the temperament of the climate in which we dwell, have upon the
exercise of our faculties, and on the character of our dispositions and turn of mind.
You will, therefore, suffer me to begin
with describing the climate of England,
and some remarkable effects, for which I
can discover no efficient cause more plain
or natural.

In the first place, a distinguishable characteristic of the climate of this island is,
its very great variableness, and a considerable degree of humidity. Winds, from
whatever quarter they blow, bring with
them rain; and in the fairest days it is very
seldom that the air is not loaded with vapours, more or less perceptible. We are
every-

everywhere enveloped in a fog; and, of
all the countries I have ever travelled in,
never did I find fogs so frequent, or so
thick and heavy. This is surely the land
of mists and vapours; and, were it not for
high winds which every now and then
sweep and dry the earth, it would be constantly damp and wet; for it is easy to imagine that the rays of the sun, having to
force a passage constantly through such a
dense atmosphere, must be greatly weakened in power and activity. I will not say
with the Marquis de Caraccioli, that *the
brightest sunshine in England is not equal to
the brilliancy of a moonlight night in Naples;*
it is, however, very certain, that the sun
appears very seldom in his full splendour:
for, when you suppose you are going to
enjoy the comfort of his beams, he is, in
a moment after, hid from you by impene-
trable clouds; and, in general, for whatever cause I know not, except it be a
peculiar predilection for the immortal
Newton and his disciples, nature appears to
be here more lavish of brilliant nights than
fair

fair days. Young, so harshly apostrophized by Le Mierre, in his *Fastes*; this Young, I say, *(Noctambule pressé que le soleil se couche,)* " the night-walker, eager to see the setting sun," considering the partial distribution of day and night in his country, had more reason for hating daylight than is generally believed.

I am sensible that these remarks apply rather to London than other parts of England. The immense consumption of sea-coal increases the quantity of fog, thickens it, and renders it of longer duration, and, moreover, causes these mists to be more gloomy and suffocating. I am never so much incommoded as at the moment I rise from my bed To breathe the fresh air of the morning is a sort of luxury which is not to be enjoyed in this noble large city, it is a poetical fancy conceived, like other felicities of the Golden Age, in the brain of the writers of eclogues. I am of opinion, that it is from being deprived of this enjoyment, that we may account for the habit so common with the English, of rising later

than

than we are accustomed to do. They will endeavour to persuade you here, that these exhalations being impregnated with nitre and sulphur, are so far from being prejudicial, that they neutralize the fogs, purify the air, and preserve it in a proper degree of temperature This may possibly be, but it is very certain they render the atmosphere thicker, and more dark and heavy, and perceptibly charge the air you breathe with a very disagreeable black smoke.

As a proof that the climate throughout England does not greatly differ from that of London, except in the circumstance just before mentioned, we may instance the nature of its produce By an excellent mode of cultivation, the land is made to produce the best of corn, and in such abundant crops that one year's harvest is sufficient for the consumption of fourteen months; the pasturage is rich, potatoes are superior to any grown in France, and hops are very good, but grapes, and all the fruits and pulse, which owe their perfection to the genial influence of a warm sun, are not to be had; it is only by mere dint of art that they are raised; and their vegetation being factitious, they have rather the resemblance than the reality of what they are called.   It is very easy to discover the great labour and painful industry which luxury employs in effecting this imposition upon itself; it is Vulcan endeavouring to get the better of Apollo, and it must be confessed, the gods themselves are apt to fail whenever they attempt any thing out of their province.

A sky in which no cloud is to be seen, is so great a novelty, that it takes place of all other news; and it is impossible for a foreigner not to remark the joyful congratulations which he hears on all sides, when the sun condescends to show himself ever so little—*a very fine day—very fine weather, indeed !*

Is it not from the uncommonness of fine weather in England that the country has produced so many good poets and so few painters of excellence? Nature is rarely seen there in her best dress. How much

more

more sensible and lively then must the imagination prove? Nature, in the perfection of her charms, is a mistress only seen in this island for a short time, and, as it were, in secret; in other countries, as in Switzerland, Italy, and in the southern parts of France, she is a wife, and her beauty is less thought of and admired. Lively impressions may form a great poet, but they will not make great painters. Because, it is not enough that the painter is strongly charmed, but he must copy nature with the pencil in his hand; he requires the advantage of time for observation; he must consider his model at leisure, he must have serene weather to view it in, and a perfect daylight to see clearly every object of his imitation; it is only under a clear sky that colours appear in their full truth and lustre.

If you were told of an island in a certain latitude, in which the winds were extremely variable, the climate rather temperate, but the air almost continually loaded with fogs and watery mists; if you were further informed

informed, that the inhabitants of this island, after having, by their labour and industry, acquired a competency, indulged in habits which induced a necessity for an abundant diet; that, indeed, they consumed little bread, an aliment which is easily changed to chyle, but a great deal of flesh, much butter, and large quantities of potatoes, and that their constant beverage was a strong * beer of a peculiar fattening quality, and in which a little opium was infused; would you not be inclined to pronounce, that with such a regimen, in such a climate, the men must, in general, have much bodily substance, and materials for life and reproduction, and, in many respects, great

---

* The very great consumption of beer in England is easily computed from the produce of the tax imposed on it. This branch of the revenue is equivalent to the land-tax, and even exceeds it, if you take into the account the duties on malt and hops In 1788, the tax on beer produced 1,666,152l sterling; besides which, there are a great number of rich individuals who brew for the use of their families, without paying any tax for the beer so consumed

strength

strength and vigour for action, and the support of labour and hardships; but that for
the most part their fibres must be soft and
flaccid, and consequently without elasticity
and feeling; and, that with a few exceptions, their animal spirits were dull, and
circulated but slowly? Well, now, what
you would presume, I think I have seen.

The English caricatures always picture a
Frenchman lean and half starved; and it
cannot be denied but that the English, in
general, have the appearance of being far
better fed This does not altogether proceed from their eating more, but from the
difference of the aliments, which the one
and the other nation accustoms itself to.
There is more gross and elementary matter
in the English diet; ours is at the same time
less heavy, and of a more bracing quality,
consequently it must more easily cherish
the warmth of the vital principle, and ac-
celerate the circulation of the blood. It is
impossible but from excess of the former
regimen there must be produced in the
moral character a greater degree of hea-

L   viness,

viness, indolence and melancholy; and by
abuse of the latter, much gaiety, folly and
precipitance.

Is not the disease to which the English
are particularly subject, and which has
passed to other nations by the name they
have given it, *the spleen*, a plain proof of
the two-fold effects of their diet and climate? Do but ask our friend Montaigne,
whether, constantly to look up to a sky
obscured with clouds and vapour, will not
dispose the mind to gloomy thoughts, and
melancholy ideas? It is not always, however, the case, that serene skies will relieve
this malady, since it was in the fine climate
of Montpelier that Lord Clive *, tired of
being the richest subject in Europe, dis-
charged the contents of a pistol against his
own head.

As a relief from the anxiety and languor,
the natural consequence of the mode of

---

* The author is here most certainly mistaken both as to
place and *instrument* —The Translator

living

living I have described, the English are
under the necessity of having recourse to
various means, which are not without
many inconveniences. They drink a great
deal of tea; this certainly helps digestion,
and dissolves the humours by helping them
in their passage, but it increases perspira-
tion, and brings on relaxations of the ner-
vous system. Another means made use of,
still more dangerous, is the habit of drinking immoderate quantities of the strongest
wines, and the most fiery spirits. Gin and
brandy are the regale of the lower sort of
people, and the women of this class are not
less addicted to drinking these liquors than
the men.

From these meteorological and dietetic
remarks, I wish to draw a conclusion which,
in my opinion, will fully explain why the
characteristic of the English is that of method and steadiness, with less restlessness
and more seriousness than we appear to
possess; an activity less lively than ours,
but more sedate; a degree of mirth less
natural than with us, but not so easily ex-

cited,

cited, nor so violent in its paroxysms; a
temper of mind less volatile, but more solid
and profound; feelings less discoverable and
active, but stronger and more just If an
Englishman begins to act he does it after
reflexion, and a full examination. His
moments of mirth and jollity convey the
idea of that sort of delirium attendant on
the attacks of a feverish disorder. Who is
there in France without wit and humour?
I will freely pronounce that the very fools
and ideots are not without it But here,
though the people in general think properly and justly on all occasions, you find
but few who are possessed of wit, except
some men of talents who, by an assiduous
attention, have opened the stores of ingenuity. Wit is not here a parasite plant,
the spontaneous production of the land; it
springs up only where it has been carefully
planted in a soil properly prepared to receive it. There is, if you will permit me
the remark, less wit and humour in England than in France; but what is found
here is more original, and better digested;
there

there are fewer false pretensions to a refined understanding here; it is here, too,
less common to apply it to an improper
use, and it is not, as in some other places,
a general received opinion, that wit can
make up for all deficiencies, and that with
it, decided opinions may be given on all
matters without study, or the least previous
acquaintance with the subject —Now let
us discourse a little on the present posture
of affairs here.

The English government, as well as that
of other countries could not behold without apprehensions the heavy storm that
threatened to set Europe in a blaze, or to
illumine it, which if England weathers, it
is less owing to the strength of its constitution than the skill, address, or good fortune
of its administration There is only the
prudence, or, if I may be allowed the expression, the natural lead of the English
character, only the usual wisdom and capacity of the Ministry that can defend this
happy country in the present juncture
against the mischievous effects of democra-

tic principles,   The longer I consider the
principles of this government and their
mode of application in its effects, the more
I perceive the truth of the observation made
to me very lately in a letter from the
B. de G.; " the prosperity of England,"
says he, " depends upon the energy and
good sense of the public character of the
nation, and, above all, upon the strength
which this character communicates to Administration, which, if weak, will not be
able to support itself "

The notions which have lately started up
in France are of so flattering and seductive
a nature that, joined with the most secret
and violent passions of the human mind,
they appear irresistible in their progress.
Whilst the words *liberty* and *equality* remain undefined, the greater is the magic
of them when uttered.   French liberty is
so remote from the freedom of all other
known governments, that the difference
which constitutes the advantages which the
English constitution has over it is lost in
the immensity of the distance.   Considering

ing the matter after this manner, I am not surprised to find an inclination generally spread over this country for adopting revolutionary principles; it prevails in every class of the people, not excepting even that which should seem from interest to have the greatest reason to dread its effects.

Certainly every one does not wish for a revolution to the same extent, nor for the same purpose. The rich landholders and the wealthy citizens wish only for some useful reform in the mode of national representation, in the manner of levying the taxes, or in laying duties on exports and imports; for a reduction or abolition of the emoluments of many places and employments without use, or which are *sinecures*, or for regulations in the law department to render their proceedings less expensive and vexatious. But how can it be ascertained that the only method of obtaining the first reform will not infallibly open a door to demands of still further extent and louder acclamation? Can a single discussion, leading to the great question of national sove-

L 4   reignty,

reignty, ever take place without danger of overturning the whole system of the body politic?

Notwithstanding this, they talk, read, and dream of nothing but revolution here as well as in France, those who have their apprehensions concerning it, and those who wish for it, are equally sanguine on the subject. The number of books, pamphlets, and caricatures, respecting the French revolution, published here within the last eighteen months, are beyond conception. Amongst the former, I must particularly notice the writings of Thomas Paine*, who

had

---

* There is no writer who has dared to attack the principles of monarchical and aristocratical governments with the freedom of this man, nor have the works of any author been more widely dispersed throughout England and America Of his *Common Sense*, more than one hundred thousand copies have been sold, and the editions of the *Rights of Man* are scarcely less numerous His mode of argument is neither so close or deep as that of the Abbé Sieyes, but his rhetoric being simple and plain, and well adapted to the understanding of the people, is capable of greater effect It has been said that he served an apprenticeship

had so large a share in the American revolution The success of his *Rights of
Man* can only be compared with the early
productions of Emanuel Sieyes. There
are only two newspapers which professedly
avow revolutionary principles, these are
the *Morning Chronicle* and the *Gazetteer*;
but the others, to gratify their customers,
find themselves under the necessity of giving a full account of affairs in France. Thus
the papers which are against the French
proceedings, as well as those which favour
them are continually furnishing the nation
with accounts that may astonish, interest,
or mislead the people There is only the
Court Gazette which observes a profound
silence about these matters.

The English people are in reality too
sagacious and prudent not to be sensible of
the advantages they have enjoyed for more
than a century through their constitution.

---

ticeship to a *Stay-maker*, but he himself acknowledges
that he studied the rights of nature and political justice on
board a privateer.

I can-

I cannot doubt but they still preserve a considerable degree of attachment to it, but they certainly do not entertain the same veneration for it, nor do they any longer idolize it. The words *King* and *Church*, which they had rendered sacred, no longer sound so delightfully in their ears; they have connected them with the word *Taxes*, and they have lost in some measure their power to charm. At the theatres, indeed, *God save the King* is constantly applauded, but those horrid words, *no King, no Parliament*, have been found written in large characters on the walls at the corner of streets more than once, and have been read without any great degree of indignation and astonishment. Thomas Paine, in one of his incendiary pamphlets, has openly declared that there can be no hopes of a thorough reform in England if recourse is not had to the only means that can save the people, a national convention.

In the present situation of affairs two circumstances must have great influence over revolutionary principles, which are

the

the vast increase of that class of the people, the men of independent fortunes, and the great numbers of men who are more or less enlightened. Formerly the rich was further removed from the poor; knowledge and information stood aloof from ignorance. The poor are more galled and hurt in every respect in which they are capable of being so by those hateful distinctions of riches and poverty

These are the natural consequences of the extraordinary progress made by industry and trade; of the invention of printing, and of the frequent recourse had to the press, of crowding men in large cities, and of the great facility of circulating notions by the esteem some languages are held in, which are thereby in a manner become common to all Europe.

The circulating cash, which is the existing mass of wealth has been diverted from its former channels The manner in which this mass is distributed has discovered more or less of its agreeable or unpleasant effects. The gold which is showered down

by

by means of the increase of commerce and
the public debts, and by the numerous
species of manufactures, is not gathered up
as heretofore   A larger proportion of individuals has been able to collect this poi-
sonous manna; the variety of comforts
which it has been the means of procuring,
has excited a greater degree of avidity, and
they who have not been able to come at a
portion of it, have discovered much im-
patience and dissatisfaction on that account.

From these several data, general as well
as particular, you will, perhaps, suppose
that every thing in this country tends to
bring about a great revolution   I shall
leave it to your own judgment to put what
construction you think proper on the circumstances which persuade me to the contrary.

The administration is in as perfect union
here, as that of France was the contrary,
at the commencement of the year 1789.
The Opposition will not pursue its former
steps but with the utmost care and caution.
There

Theie are many more people who hold pioperty here than in Fiance; and public spirit affords men heie the custom and frequent means of uniting for their real interests.

The number of poor is certainly very consideiable; but the money raised for their support is equally great. The population of England scarcely exceeds seven millions; of the three kingdoms taken together, eleven millions; and the poor's rate amounts to seventy-two millions* of French livres, exclusive of the several charities, and rich endowments, public as well as piivate, *workhouses* and poor-houses, besides establishments of gratuitous education, *fellowships, scholaiships,* &c.

Eveiy one who is in possession of any property perceives that England has not the

---

same

same faculties or power, and still fewer extraordinary resources, than France had at command, to bear up against the alarming dangers of a political subversion. Under such a violent convulsion, what would become of the public debt, that delusive phantom of an immense national credit?

The violence, or cruelty, of the English populace, is not much dreaded; but were they once to throw off all restraint, there would be great danger, from their disposition to plunder.

Though the superstitious veneration in which the constitution has been held, is attacked by certain writings, there have lately started up a number of associations, of every kind, in its defence.

The constituted authorities have preserved their full energy and activity, and they are thoroughly well disposed to aid and support government.

I must tell you plainly, that the atrocities committed in the months of August and September, have made a great alteration in the regard which was had for the

new

new order of things; but these unfavoura-
ble impressions have been nearly effaced
by the unexpected turn of fortune, in the
late brilliant successes of your * arms.
How-

---

* Now that events have shown the horrid consequences
of the first measures which were risked, from a spirit of
revolution, it appears to be inconceivable, that the European governments did not sooner discover the enormous
strength, which the establishment of national guards,
and the creation of paper money, such as assignats,
would confer on the French empire. The first of these
means certainly threw most difficult obstacles in the way of
the regular progress of a good administration of affairs, and
the maintenance of perfect order, but, when any grand
crisis presented itself, the people were prepared, at a moment's call, to rise in a mass, and an entire nation of soldiers were opposed to an army of mercenaries, collected
together with infinite pains and expence And this entire
nation of soldiers is the most populous nation of Europe,
it is true, the men are not well disciplined, but they soon
become inured to war, and their great numbers, their natural gallantry, and their promptness to a kind of enthusiasm, may well supply the want of discipline. By the creation of assignats, all the difficulties and embarrassment,
which, in a state of war, the finances of a nation are en-
cumbered with, were removed, and the necessity avoided
of the tedious and troublesome measures of loans and taxes
This operation, though fatal to property, trade and industry,

However, I fear stronger impressions, to
your prejudice, will be made by some of
your

_____

try, provided for all the exigences of war ; since by virtue of
this cruel talisman, all the riches of France, whether real or
fictitious, were thrown into circulation, and fell under the
disposition of the popular will, to be employed according to
the good pleasure of the nation.   Thus, by these two grand
measures, the genius of revolution was enabled to con-
centrate a mass of immense force, to direct it at will, and
to oppose it to all the effects of the coalesced powers, and to
defeat the calculations of their military and financial systems   These measures, at the same time that they gave
the government of France a kind of supernatural power of
action, were the unfortunate means of depriving other
governments, at war with that nation, of a great part of
their usual resources.   For, as the one government stuck at
nothing, other governments grew more than usually reserved and timorous, from the apprehension of rousing
opinions on which depended their internal quiet, and which
the universal dissemination of French principles rendered
daily more and more alarming and hazardous.   Judging
imperfectly of the unavoidable consequences of the new
order of things, our neighbours have been misled by the Con-
stituent Assembly, which was itself grossly deceived by the
artful treachery of its leading members.   It was actually
believed, that when France was no longer a monarchy, she
would become less formidable to the neighbouring nations ,
and this was credited, because it had been declared, that all
wars should be at an end.   And this idea was pertinaciously
maintained

your new laws, which no policy in the world can show to be either just or humane; more especially so; if these violent measures do not preserve you from the horrors of anarchy, which so many circumstances have, unfortunately, prolonged, and which may, in the end; be undoubtedly attributed to the nature of your principles.

A wealthy merchant, in the city, observed to me, that what might keep this country for a long time clear of the troubles which France has been involved in, is, the different character of the two nations. A Frenchman, says he, is always eager to push himself foremost; whatever may be his abilities, his confidence is very great, and he stops at nothing; an English-

---

maintained, notwithstanding it was easy to see, that from the nature of things, a great republic would be under the necessity of becoming warlike, and making conquests, foreign wars being the only means of preserving domestic peace, and at the same time of venting those passions which arise from the dangerous associations of too much power, and too much liberty

M

man,

man, on the contrary, however conscious of his own merit, has constantly, from habit, a certain caution, and a greater diffidence of himself.

Your successes in Germany have hitherto only afforded much admiration and astonishment, should they be carried further, they may, perhaps, excite other sensations.

What would be the effects of a war in which the pride and interest of the nation appeared to be equally concerned, must likewise be taken into consideration.

LET-

LETTER XII.

OF SEACOAL, AND ITS MORAL AND PHYSICAL EFFECTS.

IT is very certain, my dear sir, that in the art of writing, as in those of thinking and painting, the great difficulty consists in exposing things exactly as they are, without adding or diminishing. I am far from flattering myself that I have often hit upon this true medium, but do not charge me with representations grosser than those I have made. I have never presumed to say, that the sun was absolutely at variance with England; I may have, indeed, asserted, that the god of day seemed to have no great predilection for this country, that he was not violently fond of it, and that he was, moreover, at times, out of humour with it for a long while together. It is probable that he may dislike that constant cloud of smoke and fog with which it

is enveloped; and, I cannot but acknowledge, notwithstanding the regard I have
for this land of liberty and philosophy, that
I should like it better were it less foggy and
smoky. My last letter was full of fog,
you will find this filled with smoke.

Every thing has its advantages and its
inconveniences: I am inclined to think
that coals are a fuel which produce a
greater heat than wood, and at a less expence. It is possible that a coal fire, being more constant, more lasting and powerful, may, at the same time be more
proper to overcome the great moisture of
the atmosphere, and, therefore, absolutely
necessary in a climate like that of England.
But I shall, at the same time, take the
liberty of observing, that these sort of fires,
are neither so cheerful or brisk as ours of
wood; besides, that the form of the chim-
ney necessary for them, is neither pleasant
nor convenient, at least for the purpose of
warming the hands and feet, the extremities of the body most susceptible of the
effects of cold and moisture. There may
be

be strong objections in your opinion; but
in my mind there are others still stronger.
Physicians may, if they please, tell me,
that nothing is more wholesome, than the
sulphureous exhalations which we constantly breathe in London; for my part, I
do not perceive that colds and consump-
tions are less common here than in
other places; on the contrary, I have
thought they are more so; but I am not
able to dispute this point with them. The
only remark which I shall at present make
is, that it appears to me scarcely possible
that the eyes, the nose, the mouth, the
ears, organs of our senses continually surrounded with this black smoak, which is
of the most subtile and insinuating nature,
should not be more or less sensibly affected
by it. And in my opinion, an observation
may be easily made of the effects it has on
the membranes liable to be effected by it,
if, when care is not taken to extinguish a
fire made in your bedchamber, on going
to rest, you notice the uneasiness in your
throat on awaking the next morning. You

may

may laugh at me, my dear friend, as
much as you will, and you may charge me
with being whimsical and over nice, but
you will never remove the firm opinion I
retain, that the sensibility bestowed by nature on such minute fibres and delicate
nerves, when acted upon by the caustic
vapour of seacoal in the slightest degree,
will not, in length of time, be destroyed,
and the parts themselves become divested
of their energy and power. And is not
the possibility of such a presumption fully
confirmed by experiment, better accounted
for by this than any other hypothesis * ?

Call to mind, my dear Sir, all I have
already related of the taste, the mode of
living, the customs and manners of this

---

* The author alludes, perhaps, to an observation made
by some French writers, that iron work, in London, exposed to the open air, is, notwithstanding its being covered
with paint much corroded, which he supposes to be occasioned by this quality in the smoke of seacoal, but, in
answer to this, it may be objected, that caustics which violently affect some substances, lose their force when applied
to others —The Translator

country.

country. You will perceive more occupation, but less of that activity and ardour of life here than in France. The English are not so changeable, nor so easily moved; their minds receive more lasting impressions, but these impressions are not soon made; their feelings are more forcible, but less acute, and less varied. There is, most certainly, perceivable amongst them, little of that vivacity and readiness of wit, that rapid and intuitive comprehension of mind, which seems derived rather from the bounty of the nature, than the labour and exercise of the intelligent faculties. What method can you so naturally take to account for this specific difference betwixt the two nations, as by resorting to the physical causes I have before assigned, the influence of which, I think, I perceive, existing in effects less remote?

The English give the preference to such dishes as are highly seasoned; for instance, turtle soup; and, in general, their soups and ragouts are strongly flavoured with pepper, on the other hand, their *tarts and*

puddings

puddings are loaded with sugar. Their
pulse is served to table insipidly cooked,
but, indeed, they taste of it rarely, except
when under a regimen. The wines to
please them require to be either roughly
flavoured, or of a mawkish sweetness: such
are their Port wines, their Madeira and
Malmsey. The best wines which Burgundy and Champagne produce, are
thought by them too weak, unless the
merchant has dextrously mixed brandy
with them. Until they are thus prepared
they are supposed of an inferior quality
and not genuine. I could furnish more
instances of this kind, but what I have
now produced are, I think, sufficient to
prove, that with them, however physically
accute sense may appear in some matters,
in others it habitually demands a constant
excitation, and that in a great degree; and
even when not prematurely vitiated, so
common a misfortune in other countries

There is a moral sensibility which is
blended, as it were, with our senses, and
makes a part with them, in a manner not
to

to be resisted, it is the particular cast of this sensibility which predominates over our early attachments and the first emotions of our minds From every observation which I have been enabled to make, this kind of sensibility is less prevalent with the English than with us; and without denying the possibility of an influence from other causes, I cannot help attributing these effects in a great measure to the smoke of seacoal. What convinces me the more of the possibility of this influence is, that a moral sensibility more remote and independent of the empire of sense is discovered amongst this people of a purer, more delicate, more energetic, and chaster nature than amongst any other. Under the sanction of a more reflecting and discreet temper of mind, with public morals more strict and prudent, with prejudices respectable in as much as they support the weakness of human nature, I consider this moral sensibility less corrupted and less capable of being so. These people are honourably distinguished by sentiments of decorum, huma-

manity and uprightness, by private attachments and universal benevolence, by affec-
tions of every gentle, constant and generous kind which the heart is capable of
feeling. I will not seek for this disposition in their romances, their heroes of the
age of chivalry, nor in the manners and
actions of what has been heretofore styled
good company, but I will look for it amidst
the scenes of domestic life, and amongst
the lower classes of the people. The
lowest order of females, those who are reduced to offer their charms, or more properly their favours, to the first person who
solicits them, observe a decency and degree of modesty not to be found amongst
the same class in any other country I
have met with young men who have been
astonished at it, and some veterans in de-
bauchery who have made it matter of complaint Though frequent quarrels arise
amongst the populace, murders are very
rarely the consequence. The point of honour is strictly observed in boxing matches,
by which these disputes are usually decided;

cided; and no unfair advantage is taken of
an adversary who yields, or receives a fall;
the resentment of the victor immediately
subsides with the humiliation of his anta-
gonist, and should the former be inclined
to exercise the superiority of his strength to
the injury of the latter, the standers-by
would not fail to punish such a flagrant in-
fringement of the laws of boxing. In opposition to this instance of feeling and humanity you will perhaps object the barbarous scenes which frequently are presented on elections of members for parliament. I fear you have rather puzzled me
for an answer—these are the orgies of liberty, the transitory ebullitions of delirium
in the majesty of the mob, and by no
means their constant temper of mind. Shall
I be allowed to add that nothing can more
strongly prove that the people at large, ever
prone to these paroxysms of rage, are not
fit to be trusted with the administration of
the powers of government? As it were to
be wished that all sovereigns should prove
a Vespasian, or a Marcus Aurelius, would it

not

not likewise be desirable that no people should have the administration of their own government unless they resembled the Houynhoums or Troglodytae * ?

But to return—The first English tragedy I saw in London was Romeo and Juliet. This piece abounds with monstrous absurdities and striking beauties, as do the other capital productions of the same author. It was however an interesting performance, and many of the scenes were truly pathetic. Mrs. Esten played, for the first time, the charming part of Juliet. If her manner of representing the character was not always just, still her youth and beauty, the sweetness of her voice, and the clearness of her tones delighted the auditor. I thought her admirable in the fine scene of the second act, when she says to her lover,

> Romeo, doff thy name,
> And for that name, which is no part of thee,
> Take all myself

---

* A people of Ethiopia, so called from their living in caves.—Translator.

Though

Though my attention was fully taken up with the play and the actress, it was not so much so as to prevent me casting my eyes about me. What a disparity betwixt the melancholy silence which reigned here and the agitation of sympathetic feelings which appear in our theatres! My surprise at discovering so few emotions of concern in the countenances of the spectators, was withheld by observing a young person of a very striking figure who appeared to me the more amiable as she paid great attention to what was passing on the stage. This lovely creature seemed as insensible as the rest, and I began to tax her in my mind with want of feeling, when all of a sudden she fell breathless into the arms of a young gentleman who sat next her. No doubt she had stifled the agitation of her breast till nature was overpowered with the efforts she made to refrain from tears. This happened at the conclusion of the tragedy when Juliet exclaims, throwing herself on the body of her husband :

Stay,

Stay, stay for me Romeo,
A moment stay, fate marries us in death,
And we are one, no pow r shall part us

Be assured, my friend, that had this sweet
girl never inspired the fumes of seacoal,
her tears would have flowed sooner than
they did, and the oppression of her breast
would not have been so violent: her feelings might not have been more real, but
they would have been more tender and expressive.

As there is a species of moral sensibility
more particularly belonging to the natural
impression of the senses, the understanding
is, undoubtedly, immediately within its influence; and I cannot help thinking but
that degree of wit and judgment which we
style taste is more commonly found, and is
more capable of being improved with a
man possessed of very acute senses, than
with one who has received from nature a
different organization, or whose habits of
life or other circumstances have blunted
their delicacy.   I have been always much
pleased

pleased with the phrase used by the Romans to express a man of taste, they called him *homo emunctae naris.* Horace has made more use of this phrase than any other writer. Now, tell me how you will apply the expression to a man with the handsomest nose in the world, if it is plugged up with fog and smoke. Snuff is filthy; I grant it, but it produces contrary effects; so far from blunting the irritability of the fibres, it sharpens and quickens them.

Compare impartially the best productions of our literature with the capital works of ancient Greece and Rome, though I am far from giving them every exclusive merit, yet will you not discover a correcter and purer taste in them than in the best authors England has produced? This purity, elegance and refinement of taste, I confess, has often degenerated into a monotonous weakness, our compositions have thereby become less bold and original, but the truth of the observation is nevertheless substantiated, and that is sufficient.

ficient to justify any splenetic humour in
making it.   You shall call it idle and
ridiculous if you please; I think it really
philosophical; but I will teaze you no
longer.

LETTER

LETTER XIII

SECOND DESCRIPTION OF LONDON.

YOU know, my good friend, that my
first letters describing England, were the
productions of incessant study, and an examination pursued with the most unre-
mitting labour for the space of—a fortnight.
Do not tell me that the time is nothing to
the purpose, I am well convinced, at present,
that with respect to certain matters, time is
of consequence   For the whole fortnight
that I was in London before, it was the
finest weather possible; during four months
that I have now been detained here by a
series of unfortunate events, I have never
had sight of the sun more than a dozen
times   It can hardly happen but that this
variation of the weather must have an extraordinary effect on the appearance of a
city or country, and, consequently, the

description of a traveller of irritable feelings must be influenced by it. You may have already perceived it from my two last letters—I see London, however, on the whole, with the same eyes

The great extent of its circuit is astonishing *; no city can compare with it for the wealth and active industry of its inhabitants, for the general disposition of the *streets, roads, lanes* and *footways,* or for the number and beauty of the *squares, places* and *fields*† Whenever, by chance, the sun

---

* What adds greatly to the surprising extent of London, is the number of places surrounding it, which are themselves separately large and beautiful towns , such as Kensington, Chelsea, Clapham, &c Epsom, distant twenty miles from the capital, where there is horse-racing twice or thrice in a year, is, all the way to it, one continued suburb.

† *Roads,* are streets built upon what have been, formerly, highways , *Rows,* are houses arranged in a single line *Lanes* and *courts,* are passages through which no carriages can pass, and, therefore, they are commonly paved in the same manner as the footways *Squares,* are spaces of a quadrangular form, and *fields,* were either formerly gardens, or what their names imply

15.

is pleased to favour this vast city with the benefit of a bright horizon, there can be no situation in it more agreeable and pleasant than on the side of one of these magnificent squares, the large areas of which are generally ornamented with grass-plots of the most delightful verdure, or with clumps of shrubs and evergreens, disposed in a taste of natural negligence, both of them objects exceedingly grateful to the sight. Many of the squares are, besides, adorned with basons or fountains of water. It may appear matter of regret undoubtedly, that there are no pieces of architecture or sculpture, analogous to the design, placed in them, to embellish these charming conveniencies; but such ornaments, if admitted, must have been rigidly chaste not to have presented a disgustful contrast to the extraordinary simplicity of the surrounding buildings. The statues with which some of the squares are decorated, would appear to have little merit in the estimation of an artist, and that which is this moment before my eyes, all covered

as

as it is with gilding, would not much excite the admiration of a lover of the arts *

To form an idea of the extent of London, you must make the circuit which I
took yesterday.   Begin it from Piccadilly,
go down the Haymarket, and along the
Strand, pass the noble church of St. Paul,
and continue the line of Cheapside and
Cornhill, and make for Great Tower-hill;
then return back by that horrid street,
Thames-street, after you have taken the
refreshment of a beef-steak and some excellent pastry † opposite the Bank, pass
along

---

* In Leicester fields   A more remarkable statue than
this, is that of Charles the First, at Charing-cross, concerning which there is this anecdote remaining — After the be-
heading of that unfortunate prince, this equestrian statue,
which had been at that time set up, was taken from its pedestal
and sold to the best bidder   It fell into the hands of a
founder, who buried it in his cellar, and afterwards made a
considerable fortune by the sale of candlesticks, which, he
pretended, were cast from, and part of the same metal   At
the Restoration, Charles the Second was highly delighted
to recover the statue, and rewarded the founder in a royal
manner

† If the English are but little consumers of bread, they
make

along the Old Bailey and through Holborn to that noble street called Oxford-street, then cross Portman-square, and finish this long walk with viewing the Circus now building near Tyburn Turnpike *

---

make up for it by a vast consumption of pastry You can scarcely walk an hundred yards in the streets of London, without meeting with one or two shops full of different sorts of pastry, particularly tartlets of raspberries, currants, and gooseberries, cheesecakes, gingerbread, and cakes stuck full of corinths, with glasses filled with a clear jelly, all arranged in the neatest order, and with the utmost attention to cleanliness I have seen men and women of every rank and all ages, go into the shops in the morning and eat half a dozen of these tartlets before they went out

* The circumference of London is computed to be about thirty-six miles, but, if we allow for a number of projecting points, betwixt which there are several void spaces, this computation will be reduced to twenty-three or twenty-six miles, something more than eight French leagues. With this immense city must be included the city of Westminster, and the Borough of Southwark, with about forty-five villages, the names of which are preserved in the different quarters wherein they are situate. The increase within the course of one hundred and twenty years has been about thirty-three miles The quarter built on the other side of Black-Friars-bridge, is situated in a different county from the rest of the capital.

N 3

On

On the next morning you may find, as
I did, that you had taken too long a walk,
but you would readily admit, that there is
no city * in the world in which you could
have gone so far on foot without being ten
times more fatigued, and this is most certainly owing to the singular convenience
of footways. No person is more sensible
of the advantage of this useful introduction
than I am, and my great predilection for
populous cities makes me wish, that after
the example of London, they all would
adopt this improvement, under certain necessary restrictions On more narrowly
inspecting into this matter, however, I
can venture to hazard an opinion, that
these footways, so justly admired, were
rather intended here for the advantage of
those who dwell within the houses than
those who pass by them In general, the
houses here are not so lofty as in Paris, but

---

* We might except the city of Berne, with its magnificent piazzas, if Berne were a larger city.

they

they have greater depth underneath them;
and, I believe, I do not depart from truth,
when I tell you, that one third of the inhabitants of London live under ground
From this very circumstance, you will
readily comprehend the necessity of a
rampart betwixt the carriage-way and these
cavities, some deeper than others, which
are directly under every house. These
ramparts form the footway, raised about
four or five inches, and are of unequal
width; in the little streets they are not
more than a foot broad, and from that to
fifteen or eighteen inches, but in Oxford-
street they are above six feet wide. The
flag-stones which cover these footways are
large and smooth; and, as there is a tax imposed on housekeepers for the pavements,
they are constantly repaired as there becomes a necessity; so that you may walk
along the streets with as much ease as in
your chamber, and, except in rainy weather, nearly as little incommoded with
dirt. But you must be careful not to forget, as you are passing along, that you ap-

N 4   proach,

proach, every moment, the brink of a pre-
cipice.   Here it is a hole of some coal-
vault, there the passage, or rather stairs,
into a kitchen, work-shop, or cellar for
goods; or where wine, beer, or cider are
sold.   These little abysses are sometimes
shut up with an aukward kind of rail, or
ill made door, but in the day time are for
the most part open; and the danger of
stumbling into these pitfalls is the greater
as some of them advance further on the
pavement than others.   It appears to me
impossible, with such a defect in the mode
of building, but that many accidents must
happen in streets that are most frequented;
if they do not, the Londoners must certainly be the most attentive and quick-
sighted of any people upon earth.   But
what inclines me to think the inhabitants of
this city are not more happy in this respect
than those of other great towns, is, that I
have no where seen more wooden legs, or
persons who have lost an arm, and amongst
those cripples I observe many females
It is true the surgeons of this country are

charged

charged with a deficiency of skill in their profession, perhaps, they find it easier to amputate than to set a fractured limb. How much unlike my worthy friend Mr. John Hunter *, are these gentlemen! To

---

* Mr. John Hunter, one of the most celebrated anatomists in Europe, who must not be confounded with a quack of the same name, the inventor of a famous Restorative Balsam, &c —Thus far the author —The Translator cannot here help intruding himself upon the reader—if intrusion it should be thought by a feeling reader, that he takes this opportunity of expressing the melancholy pleasure he experiences in introducing to his English readers this testimony of an ingenious foreigner to Mr Hunter's acknowledged skill and philanthropy —Oh that the Translator could now lay before his ever revered, now departed friend and benefactor, in a moment of relaxation from his severer professional studies, the author's expression of his esteem! Such happiness he once enjoyed! Nothing now is remaining but the sad reflexion that it no longer exists! He has the consolation, however, that an opportunity has happily presented itself at this present moment of thus publickly joining his tribute of esteem and veneration to that of his author!

With respect to what the author has said of the number of cripples to be met with in walking the streets of London, the Translator cannot help observing, that he is able to confirm

To his humane attention I owe the happiness at this moment of being able with

my

---

firm in a great measure from his own observation, that the
amount of wooden legs here very greatly exceeds what is
to be met with in any city of Europe he has visited it
must, therefore, necessarily have become, in this metropolis, a striking object of speculation to a foreigner of that
acuteness of remark which the ingenious author of these
letters possesses

From what cause does this extraordinary lopping of limbs,
and flourishing state of the manufacture of wooden legs
and arms proceed? Is it from the number of hospitals
opened to receive the poor and indigent, maimed by acci-
dental fractures, or lamed through disease, attended by surgeons of the first celebrity for operations, and, on that account, followed by pupils from every part of the country,
who come merely to be spectators of their method of ope-
rating, opportunities for which are daily afforded them at
these *charitable* receptacles?

In the second volume of " Medical Facts and Observations," and the first article, is a case of compound fracture
of the leg cured without amputation, though that operation
was judged necessary, but absolutely refused to be submitted to by the patient. Upon this case the reporter, a
Shropshire surgeon, draws the following conclusion
" From this and some other similar facts,' says he, " how-
" ever necessary amputation may be in great hospitals,
" it ought to be no precedent for country practice, in which
" much

my right hand * to address you in this letter. It was owing to the lively sallies of his pleasantry, and to his amiable disposition, that I was perhaps enabled to support with calmness and resignation, a misfortune

---

" much more may be expected from the resources of na-
" ture than many imagine ' The Reviewer, in the Gentleman's Magazine for May 1794, from whence this ex-
tract is made, very justly observes that this is, " a striking
" proof of the necessity there is for great deliberation in
" cases where amputation may be thought necessary "

There is a living instance that amputation is not always necessary to preserve life , and that even limbs, when surgeons consider the case the most desperate, may be saved by the simple operation of nature   A gentleman well known to many persons at the west end of the town, had the misfortune to fall out of a window into the area of his own house, and fractured one leg and the thigh bone of the other   The fractures were considered of so dangerous a kind that it was feared death would immediately follow an amputation, and the poor gentleman was left to his fate, he has, however, happily recovered, and, with the help of a crutch-stick and a high shoe, is often met taking the exercise of walking

* It should have been before observed that it was on the occasion of his breaking his right arm that the author derived the assistance from the late Mr Hunter's skill and abilities which has merited this eulogium on his part

which

which has always appeared to me as one of
the most dreadful that can befal mankind
Benevolent old man! receive now the tribute of gratitude and acknowledgment
which I was unable then to express with
justice to my feelings, Never more shall
I write a line which my heart approves
that I shall not feel myself bound to bless
your skill and humanity! ——Forgive me,
my good friend, this little apostrophe, but
should you not pardon this short digression,
I am sure you would have no regard for
me.

After having mentioned these inconveniences, and the accommodation of a footway, as circumstances peculiar to this town
of London, I must hazard a few observations on the general appearance of this metropolis, It is far from being a showy city,
I must needs own; and I shall assign two
or three strong reasons why I think so

The first of them is that the architecture
of the houses is the simplest possible, not
to say mean; and, consequently, there is a
sameness which is intolerable· now, you
know

know that uniformity is the parent of disgust. They are almost all of them built with a small brick, either red, or of a dingy yellow, equally gloomy. The windows are for the most part without frames, and generally without shutters, they have rather the appearance of small rectangular holes in the wall than windows, and, though I am no architect, I very much suspect that besides being disagreeable to the eye without side, they do not keep out the weather more within than windows of a better fashion would do.

Another mode in the construction of houses adopted here is not less heavy and dull in the opinion of a foreigner, which is, placing iron rails against almost every house   The English have indeed more reasons than one for calling their houses their *castles*   If the areas immediately before their houses require a defence of this kind, the sight of a number of heavy black iron bars is not less offensive   During the riots occasioned by Lord George Gordon's mad flights, the mob put these bars to a

very

very cruel use But there is no necessity
of recurring to that perilous crisis to discover that this practice of setting up iron
rails have a dull, clumsy appearance; perhaps gilding might make them more lively,
or painting them of a gayer colour Upon
this occasion, now, Abbé Raynal would
tell you to a crown what it costs England in
this article of iron railing; I am not, like
him, in the secret of making such calculations: but I can assure you that the consumption of iron must be amazingly great,
and I congratulate Sweden and Russia on
the occasion.

There is scarcely any part of the town
from which that noble river which tra-
verses it can be seen. There are no quays,
and if you except London-bridge, and
those of Westminster and Black-Friars,
which are really magnificent, and a few
buildings, such as the Temple and Somer-
set-Place, both banks of this delightful river
are covered with the most filthy erections,
old stabling, or the miserable huts of fishermen and watermen. Thus the part of the

town

town which appears to admit of the most ornament is entirely obstructed, and the inhabitants are shut out from the richest prospect which the happy situation of this capital is capable of affording them. Perhaps there might be apprehensions that the construction of quays would be prejudicial to the navigation of the river by impeding the landing from boats, and laying them up, or, perhaps it might be feared that the mud, which is deposited with every tide, would hinder any pleasure from being received by such a view.

However dull the circumstances I have now pointed out may render a view of this city, especially when you add to them what I have already said upon the subject of fogs and smoke, it is certain that all of them together, disagreeable as they may be, are fully compensated in more than one way, as by the extraordinary neatness of the dwellings, both within and without, by the exertions in point of commerce, and the universal industry which gives animation and spirit to every quarter of the town, added

added to the variety of merchandize of every
kind exhibited in the windows of the different shops and warehouses, displaying in
the most ingenious manner a sight of the
productions of all parts of the habitable
globe.   In short, if the observation is just
which has been made of a great city, that
it is an epitome of the whole wold, it applies with propriety to no city so much as
to London.   It was this consideration which
caused me to admire it so greatly in 1789,
and since I have viewed it again more at
my leisure, and perhaps with fewer prejudices, I am still of the same opinion in
these respects.

May these glorious monuments of European civilization escape the fury of revolutionary enthusiasm altogether; or may
they at least escape it long enough for us
to be convinced from the example of other
countries that our new systems may be ex-
celled by greater prodigies of happiness
and power!   National sovereignty, however absolute we may suppose it, can have
no pretence to exceed the limits of reason
                                            and

and justice   And is it not exceeding those limits, manifestly to sacrifice the happiness of the present generation to the chimerical hope of the quiet and happiness of future generations, which is promised with a generous confidence indeed, but at the same time a confidence not only rash but imprudent?

L E T T E R XIV.

OF THE ENGLISH STAGE.

THE theatres were amongst the things I saw most imperfectly during my first journey to England; I have this time visited them with perhaps a greater degree of attention. Mortified as I am with a number of vexations, seeing the only consolation left me removing still further and further, and sometimes entirely lost to me, discontented moreover with my present situation, and more uncertain of improving it in future, I resort to the theatre as to a place where I may find a kind of felicity, that of a lively concern for feelings not my own, and of sometimes dropping a tear which eases my breast, because it is not the tear of anguish; in a word, I seek the theatre as a spot in which I may forget myself; for, in my opinion, it is not one of the least evils attendant on calamity, that in spite

of

of all we can do it constantly recurs to our minds by the melancholy necessity we are laid under by it of paying an over degree of attention to our own concerns

I have seen since I have been here the best productions of Shakspeare, Otway, Rowe, Congreve, Cibber, Steele, Vanbrugh, and the most admired pieces which have been produced within the last twenty years, together with some new ones I have, moreover, attended Mrs. Siddons in her principal characters, and I will own to you, that having seen the English Melpomene, I think I have seen for the first time the tragic muse in all the dignity of the buskin, with all the majesty of her sceptre, and encircled with all her fascinating charms. That I may not be accused of prejudice, I must now declare that I have seen only the shattered remains of what Mademoiselle Dumesnil had been in France, and I never had the happiness to see Mademoiselle Clairon on the stage; though I had often what I cannot but think a pleasure superior to it, that I mean of living with

O 2   her,

her, and being perfectly acquainted with the charms of her wit, the nobleness of her sentiments, the strength of her mind, and of having enjoyed the inestimable felicity of a disinterested and uninterrupted friendship with her.

One of the first things that struck me in Mrs Siddons was the grandeur of her air and manner, the grace and dignity of her attitudes in every variety of character, whether it was calmness or passion that she was to represent   Though this sublime actress exceeds most women in height as she does in every other respect natural or acquired, she is without the defect common with such of her sex as are above the usual standard, that of having too long arms; a defect which always gives the actress an appearance at once aukward and ungraceful Her face is well formed and full of expression; the upper part is strongly marked with firmness and spirit, and every muscle displays those characters perfectly; perhaps with an appearance of too much harshness and force, had she not the talent of softening them

them at pleasure According to the exact
rules of proportion her nose may appear too
bold and prominent, but the eye is not at
all affected by it, because it is perfectly
well shaped, and though not agreeing with
the rest of her features, is exceedingly ac-
cordant to the grand style of her face if
considered together To be insensible of
the justice of this distinction, or to consider it as trifling and over refined, is to acknowledge an insensibility of the powers
of physiognomy; however that may be, I
think a true physiognomist would consider
it as a remarkable circumstance that with
features thus strongly marked, and a countenance of such confined harshness, nature
should have bestowed on this truly tragic
visage such an extraordinary degree of
flexibility You behold the most opposite
passions succeeding each other so rapidly,
and with such a natural transition, as is really
wonderful and astonishing, she heightens
the passions and embellishes them, she
softens and corrects them by her com-
manding figure Even in that convulsive

O 3   laugh

laugh which precedes the death of Isabella*, in that extraordinary fit of frenzy,
but one of the most horrible and shocking
kind, she preserves all the dignity of grief
and horror of the situation which causes it,
tears, sobbing, terror, despair, desolation,
all are so far from taking from the majesty
of her person that they serve to render her
more affecting and tender.   There is a
certain force and softness of expression in
her eyes and mouth that can only be compared with the tone of her voice, which is
at once melodious, clear, articulate and
thrilling.   Twenty times did Mrs Siddons
make me forget that it was an English tragedy I saw her performing in; nay, it is

---

* Isabella, or the Fatal Marriage, a tragedy, altered
from Southern by David Garrick   Isabella, in a fit of
madness, brought on her through despair, holding the
dagger in her hand, with which she is about to stab herself, exclaims—

Biron, he steals it from the sleeping Gods, and sends it
      thus—
Now, now I laugh at you, defy you all, you tyrant-mur-
      derers

ex-

exactly the truth which I am now relating;
I saw Lady Macbeth, or Calista, or Belvidera, or Jane Shore, or Volumnia, by turns
before me, I heard them speak without
noticing in what language, whether mine,
or their own, what do I say? It was certainly their own language they spoke, but
so magical was the deception, that I know
not how it was, but it appears to me at this
moment they spoke a language which my
heart perfectly understood.

I write my own sentiments concerning
Mrs Siddons; I have asked no one's opinion of her acting. Undoubtedly I am
not singular in the account I have given
you of it; all her countrymen consider her
talents as I do, and I will add, the greater
part of such foreigners as have had occasion to see, and to criticise them. It is a
general opinion in London, that if Garrick
was the greatest actor, Mrs Siddons is the
greatest actress the English stage could ever
boast of And, having done her this justice, how can I, without great concern,
inform you that she is nearly forty years

O 4   of

of age, and that she has scarcely displayed
her extraordinary skill before a London
audience more than ten. The reason is,
that as long as Garrick lived, whether it
proceeded from prejudice or jealousy, or
from whatever other unaccountable motive,
he used all his power and influence to prevent her appearance in the capital She
is the daughter of a mean provincial actor,
but a man of good character, who took
proper care of her education, and particularly with regard to prudence and virtue
Being without fortune, and having no better
means of getting a livelihood, she offered
herself as a waiting-maid to a lady in
Warwickshire, soon after which her theatrical talents were, I know not how, discovered all at once. She did not alter her
manners in taking to this profession, her
conduct has always been decent and irre-
proachable. She is a prudent wife and a
tender mother; she is, indeed, tender to
an extreme, for on the death of a favourite
girl last year she was nearly plunging her-

self

self into so deep a melancholy as to occasion apprehensions of her loss of reason, if not of life A man who pretends to great understanding assured me the other day that he had often conversed with her but had found her discourse very insipid and without the least wit Good God! answered I, with a genius and talents like those of Mrs Siddons, do you suppose any one enquires about her wit? It is some months ago since she attempted to model Without a master, and without instructions, she has finished a bust of her brother which artists themselves view with astonishment.

I have found no actress to be compared with Mrs Siddons in tragedy If you except her brother, Mr. Kemble, in some characters, such as Coriolanus, Macbeth, and in the Merchant of Venice, all the men are in my opinion far below our St Prix and Vanhove, and the women are much the same Mrs Pope may have been handsome formerly, but she is now a precise old woman Mrs Esten is young and handsome, but her talents are still younger than

than her face, and, perhaps, may ever continue so. Mis Powel wants feeling and dignity; her mode of declamation is languid, dull, and monotonous

The English stage can at present boast of possessing comic performers of extraordinary excellence; such are Miss Farren and Mrs. Jordan. The former has great taste and elegance in her appearance, if you except a custom common with women in this country, which is that of pressing their elbows too closely behind them. She has a most lovely countenance, appears to be full of vivacity and spirit, and hits off the air of a woman of fashion exactly. It is said Lord D—— waits only for the moment he shall be at liberty to offer her his hand There is no circle, however brilliant or *fashionable*, wherein her ladyship, as she will then be styled, need fear finding herself out of her sphere The tone of her voice has naturally something of dryness and sharpness in it, but she moderates these defects by the most correct, and the exactest pronunciation. There is sometimes too much art and stiffness perceptible in her manner of acting. These faults are amply made up by a just and accurate conception of her character, and a chaste and lively performance of it. She is particularly admirable in The School for Scandal, in the character of Lady Emily in The Heiress, and in The City Wives' Confederacy. What will make you downright in love with her, is, that they tell me, she is as declared a democrat as the noble lord her sweetheart.

Mrs. Jordan's stile of acting is not so extensive, and is adapted to a smaller set of characters; yet such parts as are suitable to her talents she represents in a manner more striking and natural. Her figure is neither so genteel nor sprightly as Miss Farren's, yet she is distinguishable by a kind of graceful simplicity, and her acting is more pleasing to the audience, because it is an exact and delightful copy of pure nature. To the sweetness and natural sensibility of her voice, she has a happy manner of joining that expression of character, that smart-

ness

ness in delivering her words which makes a quick and lasting impression on the auditor. The characters in which I have seen her exhibit, with the greatest success, all the simplicity, and the charming playfulness of her talents, are, Hypolita, in She Would and She Would Not, her character in the Spoil'd Child, and that of Peggy, in the Country Girl. I shall not tell you in which of these parts Mrs Jordan effected her fascination of the Duke of Cl—; but I will assure you it is sufficient to see her in any one of them to be convinced she is possessed of a deal of witchcraft

Accustomed as I have been, for two years, to listen to the sweet melody of Mandrini, Viganoni, and Morichelli, you cannot suppose me to become a ready admirer of any merit the musical performers of this country may lay claim to   It must, however, be confessed, that the passion for music has been increasing in England for some few years.   I do not recollect having seen, since I have been this time in London, a piece wherein there was not more or less singing;

singing; over and above the favourite airs
of *God save the King* and *Rule Britannia*,
which are called for vociferously from the
galleries, the moment any musician pops
his head into the orchestra Having paro-
died some of the airs of France and Italy,
the English begin to persuade themselves
that their language is as capable of musical
expression as another; and, indeed, I find
the music of their little operas better exe-
cuted than it was three or four years ago.
The pretty Miss Storace and the celebrated
Madame Mara are never more sure of applause than when they sing English words;
and the beautiful Mrs Crouch, who never
was out of her own country, has a voice
that would be heard with pleasure on the
theatres of Rome or Naples

Mrs Bland, and Miss De Camp, have,
likewise, fine voices; but their singing appears to me to have more of the
taste of the British soil in it than that of
Mrs Crouch Incledon, Kelly, Dignum,
are all agreeable singers in their way, at
least they have the satisfaction to find themselves

selves always well received by the London
pit.

If you please to recollect what I have
often said to you of Edwin, you will imagine I was much concerned to learn, he
added one to the graves in Covent-Garden
church-yard, dying about a twelvemonth
ago, in the prime of his years. Though
I am naturally of a disposition melancholy
enough to suit the English character, yet
the death of a man remarkable for the extraordinary festivity of his mirth and talents, appeared to affect me with a degree
of sorrow I have rarely experienced on
the like occasions. The history of his life is
published here, with a collection of his jokes
and witty sayings. The actor most likely
to supply the loss of that excellent come-
dian is most certainly Bannister, junior;
but, I freely own to you, his acting has neither so much of nature, nor has it that dry
humour which Edwin's preserved. However, I will declare, that to make up for
this deficiency, he has more address, and
more grace and variety in his manner of

acting

acting. Add to this, he has a very keen eye, and the best teeth possible In The Cheats of Scapin, translated from Moliere, by Otway, his performance of the character equals that of our Preville or Feuilli. In the little Apothecary, in the Prize *, he has all the drollery of Dugazon It is a caricature which it is impossible to perform with more spirit and comic effect than he gives it.

'I have been greatly pleased with many pieces, and particularly with those in which King, Lewis, or Kemble have had characters; but I must pass many years in London before I can be reconciled to the strange figures, and still stranger grimaces, which Suett and Dodd make upon the stage Dodd is, notwithstanding his large head and great belly, the first actor in his

---

* The Prize, or A Ticket in the Lottery, is one of the prettiest after pieces which has been brought on the stage this winter The principal character is a country apothecary, whose head is turned from the notion of his having obtained the ten thousand pound prize

Majesty's

Majesty's company, for the parts of fine
gentlemen and fops; somewhat in the
manner of our marquisses and petits-maîtres,
as represented on our stage by Fleuri and
Molé.

There are certain singularities, forms and
customs, in the style of acting peculiar to
the English stage, which a foreigner is dis-
gusted with, till by use he becomes reconciled to them.   Of this sort are the bows
which every favourite actor is expected to
make to the audience as soon as he appears,
however out of character or discordant with
the situation such compliments may happen to be · then there is a kind of mecha-
nical changing of sides by concert betwixt
two actors from left to right, and from right
to left; add to these, an affectation of pro-
longing the sound of certain cries or ex-
clamations, and an emphasis, or kind of
organ stop placed upon all the *ohs* and *ahs;*
and, lastly, the frequent starts of passion
in which the performer is obliged to fall flat
upon the stage, the noise of which, being
so frequently repeated, is disagreeable

A fo-

A foreigner, especially if he be French, cannot but often find, in the declamation of the stage, something more or less of exaggeration, heaviness, violence or harshness, but after he has learned how to discriminate betwixt the faults of the actor and those which originate with the genius of the language, or the peculiar character of English poetry, he will at last be brought to confess, that these passages and movements, which at first displeased and astonished him, have an infinite degree of expression, and produce a wonderful theatrical effect. Every language has its peculiar accent, and the great merit of an orator or player consists in the happy use of it by a just and perfect accordance, not only of the accent with his pronunciation, but of his pronunciation with the action. The exact agreement of all these parts constitute the pleasure which arises from an apt and proper declamation. Thus the action of an English performer must be as different from that of an Italian or French actor, and ought to be so, as the accent of their lan-

P   guages

guages and mode of pronunciation. The relation betwixt sound and gesture is so much in nature, that you can scarcely see a man who has a bad ear but you find him very aukward in his gait and carriage

You are already acquainted with my opinion of the dramatic merit of the great Shakspeare; I find no reason to alter it; but what will puzzle you much, as it has done me, to reconcile with the religious veneration he is held in by his countrymen, is the liberty that is taken, without controul, to improve or disfigure, to amplify or abridge, his capital works. Not one of his pieces is represented on the stage as he wrote it, or as it is printed in the collection of his works. There are some so disguised as not to be discoverable for his writing, as is The Tempest, by Dryden, who has introduced into it the tale of Friar Philip's Geese In the same manner, those which Garrick has taken upon himself *to alter*, for that is the term, have undergone a number of transpositions and cuttings-out. To find out the most pathetic piece written by Shakspeare,

speare, you must limit your choice to
Othello, Romeo and Juliet, or King Lear.

According to my ideas of poetical imagination and theatrical effect, Macbeth is
productive of the greatest degree of wonder
and astonishment. You may call it, if you
please, a monstrous production, but you
will be obliged to acknowledge that there
is a richness of conception, of character,
and of invention, displayed in the greatest
exuberance, at once discovering the boldest
and most original strength of genius. You
will there see united, and with some degree
of simplicity, every species of the marvellous, history, epopœia, romance, opera
and magic, all conducing to confirm one
great moral truth, and heightening the
effect of the most tragical situation, till it is
worked up to the sublimest degree of sentiment, of terror, and of remorse. Though
this is one of the pieces in which I was most
affected by the extraordinary talents of
Mrs. Siddons and her brother, yet I cannot
say I was very much pleased with the style

P 2

in which it was represented   There is
too much meanness and false taste in the at-
tire of the witches and their group.   By
the mode in which these scenes are represented, you might be led almost to imagine that the actors wished to burlesque
them, though certainly nothing could be
more easy than to render them awful and
striking   I cannot see the propriety of
Banquo personating the character of his
own ghost, it should be through Macbeth's
fears that we should discover the apparition
which haunts him, and he should be no
more visible to the audience in the pit than
to the guests at the banquet   Mr. Kemble
has frequently wished to lay this ridiculous
ghost, but he is afraid of doing it; the galleries, he says, would stop the performance
and call out for the ghost they had been
accustomed to see ; and the ghost, after he
has risen through the trap-door upon the
stage, on receiving the thunder of applause
it would occasion, must indispensably stop
the performance still further, by returning
his

his thanks in a low bow; all which would disconcert the actor and destroy the effect of the whole scene.

The very great degree of admiration which has been had for Shakspeare's tragedies, has nearly caused his comedies to be forgotten, they are, nevertheless, to the full as wonderful in their kind; as well for the boldness as the originality of their characters, for the interest and variety of their situations, for the spirit and vivacity of the dialogue, for their abundant and natural pleasantries—pleasantries, I say, so natural, that they appear such, though replete with extravagance, and a continual play upon words. For there are some ridiculous extravagances for which the severest critic cannot help making allowances, on account of the false taste of the age. The part of Falstaff is a caricature, but there is a striking degree of nature, and a singular vein of comic humour in the character. His intrigue with the Merry Wives of Windsor, is well imagined, and full of mirth and conceit. Nothing can be more extravagant, and at the

P 3   same

same time more touching than the play of
The Merchant of Venice

There is scarcely a single theatre in London which is not of too small a size for the
full display of the representation of English
tragedy.   Of all modern theatrical productions, surely those of the English theatre
are what can best fill a stage of large di-
mensions, because I know of none which
abound in such changes of decoration, or
wherein there are so many situations that
demand great show and preparation.   How
is it that the pride of the nation has not
suggested the measure of erecting a grand
monument to the glory of the dramatic art,
a building in which the great productions,
so much the admiration of the people,
might be represented with all the splendour and magnificence for which they are
so well adapted ? It is not from an indiffer-
ence to the pleasures of this seductive art,
for, I believe, theatrical representations
have been at no time more encouraged in
France and Italy, than they are at this present moment in London.

I shall

I shall add but one observation more to
what I have already said of Shakspeare, that
as much as his tragedies are admired, they
are not those by which audiences are now
the most affected. None of his tragedies
have caused so many tears to be shed as I
have seen drop at the representation of Jane
Shore, Venice Preserved, The Grecian
Daughter, or the Gamester The critic
must entertain a strange degree of prejudice
for this great dramatist, who should presume to say, that the mixture of scenes of a
trivial and burlesque nature, which he has
introduced in his sublimest and most tragical pieces, do not diminish the effect intended to be produced by the situations of
his principal characters We find, in the
unravelling of the plot of his dramas, less
to excite our sympathy than our terror and
surprise. He has the sublime art, above all
other dramatic writers, of rivetting our attention, and filling us with astonishment.
Poets of talents, perhaps, far inferior to
his, have better understood the secret of

P 4   touch-

touching our feelings and beguiling us of our tears

In the room of going on here with an apology, which I had once undertaken to make for the licence and inconsistencies of the English stage, I should much rather refer you, in a modest manner, to one already made to my hand, by the celebrated poet Dryden, which is to be met with at the conclusion of his life written by Johnson One of the positions on which he dwells the most, is, that the taste of the English nation not being hurt by that irregularity and inconsistency which foreigners object to the best English dramatic poets, the stage evidently becomes thereby infinitely benefited, because the emotions of pity and terror being more easily excited, and by a greater number of devices, the display of these passions being speedier and more ready, the art, by these means, derives a multitude of resources, and the spectators feel a more sensible degree of pleasure. This dramatic system cannot, un-

undoubtedly, produce so thorough and continual a deception as that which made the ground-work of the admired productions of the Grecian and French stage but are deceptions of this sort very common? And that which we in reality experience during a theatrical representation, does it last beyond the duration of an act, or a scene? If the scene is all that it ought to be, will it not have the same effect whether it has been prepared at leisure, or whether it has been abruptly produced? Do you really suppose that my imagination is not as often confused in France, by the difficulty you find in connecting a couple of scenes, as it is here by the insipidity and aukwardness of interruption occasioned by a change of decoration? After having thus compromised with poet and spectator, for both being mutually spared the intricacy and fatigue of unbroken scenes, we can readily pass from one situation to another, and every thing becomes more or less dramatical I own, the scenes are, in this case, simply a succession of pictures, which

follow

follow each other, not without a degree of
disorder and irregularity, and often with
but little probability; somewhat like, if
you please, a magic lantern But the in-
terval is short which disjoins them. If the
pictures are just, if they have life and energy, and if they have a strong relation to
the action, if they unfold it in the tenderest and most expressive manner, with
warmth and rapidity, your attention is
taken up, you are continually led towards
some affecting object, and you have no
leisure for consideration of the means
whereby your eyes and all your thoughts
were captivated. How much time is lost
in the greater part of our French pieces, to
prove to the audience that the author, or
his *dramatis personæ*, were in the right to
say or do what they have done or said!
What is it to me, who am only a spectator,
whether the author can justify himself or
not? Let him commit as many faults as he
pleases, let him lay himself open to the
severity of criticism, if I am but interested;
if I am moved, and my attention excited,

at

at least, if it be excited with spirit and animation, I ask no more If any one should doubt, from what I have said, whether I do not prefer the noble tragedies of Sophocles, of Corneille, and of Racine, to the admirable monsters of the English stage, I think you will not be the person. You will discover, in the impartiality of my remarks, a desire of embracing every kind of beauty; and that the disadvantages of any particular system do not prevent me likewise, from seeing the advantages of it. The great fault of the French stage results, perhaps, from the arbitrary necessity of a regular and well-grounded conduct, for the French, in my opinion, affect, in their diversions, the appearance of rationality beyond other nations, probably with the idea of being dispensed from it in matters of more serious consequence The beauty, as well as imperfection, of the English stage, arises from the necessity of strongly exciting the passions of its audience, and constantly rousing attention, as otherwise the spectators might not be at all touched with
the

the scene. And, conforming to these two principles of writing, how shall the author avoid, in the one case, becoming vapid, spiritless, cold, and monotonous, and in the other, absurd, extravagant, abounding in irregularities and characters out of nature?

As the English delight only in tragedies which become interesting by the great strength and variety of situations, so no comedies are to their taste which do not possess great intricacy of plot, characters bold and prominent, lively and uncommon turns of wit and humour, bordering, more or less, upon buffoonery. It appears difficult to reconcile the general moral conduct for which these people are remarkable with the great immorality and indecency of their comedies You will find amongst these a great many pieces in which the characters, the manners, the strokes of wit, all seem to be borrowed from places of the most infamous resort. This arises most probably from the circumstance of their earliest successful pieces, and which have served as models of succeeding ones, having been written

written during the reign of Charles the Second, a period when the example of a court, abandonly vicious, countenanced a dissoluteness of manners, with design, undoubtedly, of relieving the Londoners from the mischiefs which the gloomy austerity of puritanical morality had brought upon them. No women but those of a particular class scarcely ever went to a play, and hardly ever without a mask before their faces I know no dramatic piece which abounds with more wit and humour than the Beggar's Opera, but I know of none at the same time which is capable of producing more dangerous or immoral effects —— Some fashionable philosophers might perhaps be of opinion, that the first scene of the second act, is one of the plainest and best declarations of the rights of man that was ever written

The modern pieces which appear to me the most striking and best pictures of the present manners, and the most perfect models of polite manners and conversation, are the School for Scandal, written by She-

Sheridan, and the Heiress of General Bur-
goyne. These two pieces have in them
all the spirit and vivacity of the old co-
medy, at least as much as is consistent with
the decorum of character, the general interest of the action, the truth of the dialogue, and the constant elegance of style.

As in my first letter on the subject of
the English stage I introduced something
about the dress of the ladies, I think I must
give you now a word more upon that matter; I think myself the rather bound to do
it, because I cannot, in conscience, but
make a solemn reparation to the *ladies of
fashion,* who condecend to adorn the theatres with their presence. The dress of
their hair, and the fashion of their cloaths
are much improved since 1789; and you
will not be surprised at what I say, when
you are informed that London at this present time has the happiness of being in
possession of the united talents of Monsieur
Leonard and Mademoiselle Bertin, not to
mention a number of French *femmes de
chambre* who have had the benefit of their
skilful

skilful instructions When I see the display of luxury, and the arts in actual wealth,
and ornamental frippery at the levee at
St James's, in Hyde-Park, and New-Bond-
Street, and at the theatres, I am in a pet;
you may call it a pet of selfishness or of patriotism, as you please, but I cannot help
thinking that all that a neighbouring power
in a fit of metaphysical lunacy has been
throwing out at window, her rival has eagerly picked up You will tell me, to be
sure, that the latter will not fail to repent
it; and at this moment I have not the
power of proving the contrary The only
thing which I shall insist upon with any
degree of obstinacy is, that, as the English
ladies are daily improving in taste, they
should altogether lay aside the use of *stays*;
I mean such as are stiffened and rise high
in the neck, because from a defect in their
form they cause an elevation of the shoulders, and a curvature in the back, which
robs the shape of all its natural ease Some
ladies, instead of these stays, have taken to
wearing girdles very broad, and fixed pretty
high This fashion which is borrowed
from

from the dress of the ladies of ancient Greece, is attended with this inconvenience, that when it is indiscreetly followed the upper part of the body appears by much too short, another inconvenience greater still attends it, which is, that it causes a prominency not consistent with that just shape, which belongs to youth and perfect health. This absurdity is carried to such an extreme that some ladies make use of artificial means to procure this kind of deformity of shape, and you may imagine what disgustful effects must be produced by following so ridiculous a fashion. This gave rise to *pads* and *padded ladies* of which you have lately read so many aukward pleasantries in the newspapers If Madame la Marquise de Deffant were living now, she would recollect upon this occasion what she observed upon the whim which Madame Châtelet suddenly took into her head, of setting off in the depth of winter to visit her husband who was at his estate in Lorraine "This extraordinary fancy," said she, "can only be the longing of a woman "with child."

LETTER

LETTER XV.

ON THE ENGLISH LANGUAGE.

YES, I am of opinion with Figaro, that it is not always necessary to be master of the subject upon which you intend to write; nay, I will go farther, I do really believe, that it is for the very reason of your not being master of it that you are sometimes able to form a better judgment. Will you not agree with me that it is not always the rich man who discourses with most propriety upon riches, neither is it he who enjoys the greatest share of health who sets the most value on that enjoyment, so neither is it the most learned men who discover the highest respect for the use and advantage of science. You will, then, not be surprised if, having acquired no more English than I had when I first arrived in London, I presume to communicate in this letter some observations which I have made

Q on

on the genius, the difficulties, the beauties, and the defects of that language. If I was as perfect a master of it as you are, perhaps I should not have made these remarks, the discriminating character of a language has a different effect upon the foreigner from what it has upon the man who has spoken it from his infancy. There is only one good reason why the English language is so easy to acquire by book, which is the extreme simplicity of its syntax That of the Hebrew, which is esteemed the simplest, as it is the most ancient speech made use of by mankind, has rules of greater intricacy. Properly speaking the English language has neither declinations nor conjugations. To distinguish the number and cases of their substantives they have only one or two terminations, the difference of which is not very great, and one or two articles, which are in reality particles, employed often to express other relations. Their adjectives are all of them neuter, and are without a plural. Their verbs have only two distinct tenses, the present and the past, and these

are

are sometimes only marked by the pronunciation, the others are formed by means
of these helping verbs, *to have, to be, to do,
shall, will, can, may, must* These all may,
without much labour, be learned in five or
six lessons. The grammar of a language,
composed of elements so simple as this,
cannot be of any great length. The relations of one word to another not being
marked in this language, either by the variety of articles as in the French, or by that
of the termination as in the Greek and
Latin, the inversions cannot be frequent,
or the style rendered obscure Whatever
of these, custom, or the particular manner
of some writers, have introduced, the intention and drift of the sentence will explain. And without doubt it proceeds from
this difficulty joined to the frequent use of
ellipsis, aphercsis, and syncope, that to understand English poetry, a particular degree of application and attention is required;
but this is a labour so well rewarded by the
pleasure and satisfaction attending it, that
it is by no means discouraging.

But

But there is one very mortifying circumstance you meet with, which is, that after
you are able to understand English in a
book tolerably well, when you hear any
one of the words you are acquainted with
pronounced, you are totally at a loss for the
meaning of it.   In reality, I know no one
language in which the orthography differs
so much from the pronunciation; nor do
I know of any in which the pronunciation
is at the same time so difficult, so uncertain, and so variable; insomuch, that it
might be supposed that the orthography
and pronunciation were of very different
and distant ages*.   Sheridan, the father of
one of the most celebrated orators of the
present times, has said, in the preface to
his dictionary, " With regard, indeed, to the
" pronunciation of our tongue, the obstacles
" are great; and, in the present state of things,
" almost insuperable "   Yet this author

---

* Madame Dennis, Voltaire's niece, said once to her
English master, " You write *bread,* and you pronounce it
" *bred,* why not say at once *du pain* ?"

saw

saw these obstacles only as they appeared
to him in the inadequate methods used for
instruction in the cultivation of the language, but are they not likewise to be met
with in its elementary composition? In
the first place, the English tongue abounds
in consonants; of which the number is
greater than is commonly marked in the
alphabet. Our *j* is pronounced *edzh* or
dzha, our *c* is sometimes pronounced hard
as a *k*, and sometimes like an *s*, and sometimes too like *sh*. T has one-while the
power of the *s*, at another time of *sh*, or *ch*,
and the like, over and above its natural
sound as *t*. Now the greater the number
of consonants in any language, the greater
is the harshness and difficulty of its pronunciation. Nor is the pronunciation softened
down, or rendered more easy, by the help
of the vowels, which are few of them of
sufficient purity or clearness of sound to
strike the ear, and arrest the attention. In
the English speech our five vowels represent from twelve to fifteen different sounds;
and some of these sounds have the disad-

Q 3   vantage

vantage of being very short or very faintly expressed, as the *a* in *hat*, the *e* in *bet*, the *i* in *fit*, the *o* in *not*, and the *u* in *but*, the others are nearly all of them pure diphthongs, which have none of them so clear or determinate a sound as the pure vowels expressed by us in the *i*, the *a*, and the *o*. To this must be added a considerable variety of words beginning with an *s*, or a *th*, which can only be properly expressed by pressing the tongue against the teeth It is very easy to conceive that a speech like this of the English, composed of such a multitude of consonants, of vowels which are surds, of uncertain diphthongs, of monosyllables, and of syllables extraordinarily short, must admit of great uncertainty and instability in its pronunciation The poor foreigner is, therefore, under the hard necessity of applying himself to the study of the practice, and the organs of all those with whom he is to converse, before he is able perfectly to understand them This calls to my recollection the distress which the B. de R. a friend of mine, was under, who

who, after taking incredible pains in pronouncing the word *sir* to the approbation of his first masters, and having changed his mode twice, was obliged to undergo a third practice in conformity to the modulation of a new instructor. Indeed, the last gave him a piece of advice which perhaps may be found very pithy and applicable to the purpose "You must endeavour," said he, "Sir, to lay your accent very strongly, and "with propriety, you are then to pronounce as gently as you please: and, my "word for it, you will be understood."

If there be a poverty, and, if I may so express myself, a degree of barbarity in the English language in respect to its elements and grammatical construction, there is at the same time a wonderful force and richness, and an abundant boldness and originality in its expression. Whatever tongue you profess to be skilled in, you will find nearly the whole of it in the dictionary of the English language. I know no language of equal extent, yet I must own I could not help being seized with a degree

Q 4 of

of apprehension and alarm when I perused
the proposals for a new edition of Johnson's
celebrated dictionary, which was to be en-
larged with an addition of upwards of
twenty thousand new words The language in which the noblest book in the
world is written, the Bible, has not more
than from seven to eight hundred , and not
more than half that number is reckoned in
all the operas of Quinaut

The English language evidently derives
its origin from the ancient Teutonic, and
the pronunciation of those primitive words
are less altered than are the words daily
borrowed from modern tongues. But the
analysis of the two languages is far from
having any affinity with each other, for
the German is as complicated and difficult
in its grammatical construction as the other
is plain and simple If there are some
Anglicisms in which the genius of the German original is to be traced, they are but
few in number *. I have no doubt but
both

---

* The German original is, however, to be discovered in
these

both idioms must sound uncouthly to the
ears of southern nations, but, to consider
them with impartiality, I think the German
language more susceptible of harmony and
numbers, the other more pliant and ma-
nageable, they are both of them naturally
energetic, but the former maintains a dull
and heavy stateliness*, the other without a
greater degree of softness, has less constraint,
and more boldness and rapidity in its progress An English lady as impartial as she
is ingenious and lively, observed to me one
day that her country music had something
in it like the sharp dry sounds produced by

---

these two English expressions—*What did we play for?*
Whom do you write to? The frequent suppression of the
pronoun relative is common to both languages

* In my opinion several reasons are to be assigned for the
tedious monotony of the German language, from its construction, from the drawling and difficult combination of
the auxiliary verbs, from the little use made of participles,
from the frequent repetition of harsh and disagreeable
sounds, such as the *oun*, the *oum*, and the *our*, and from
the great number of lengthened mute terminations, such as
en, em, and *end,* in *lieben, meinem, liebend,* and others

the

the washing tub, when laboured by the
laundresses. I made so fice as to ask her
if she did not think this comparison exactly expressed the natural melody of her
language, when not spoken by herself,
with that grace of delivery and harmony of
pronunciation which she was capable of
embellishing it with.

England seems indebted to France for
all those expressions which have relation to
the customs, ideas, and manners of society.
The English language appears indeed to
have borrowed a very great number of
words from ours; but if we are able to discover them readily in the books we peruse,
we have it not in our power to detect the
same words when we hear them pronounced: for there is scarcely one of them
cognizable, so much are they altered by
the pronunciation. There are others which
have strangely changed their signification
since crossing the Channel   I am at a loss
to assign a reason why the word *ennui*,
which has a meaning strongly expressive
and peculiar to itself, has not been honoured
                                    with

with naturalization, as well as many others from the same country. Is this disease of the mind entirely unknown in England? or is it because, in this fortunate island, people always find amusement, and never suffer from satiety, or inaptitude for enjoyment?

In my opinion there is a very striking parallel to be drawn betwixt the English language and the wealth of the nation. The stock which laid the foundation for this wealth, was not very great; but through the perseverance, activity, and industry of the nation, it has been very considerably improved, by every mode of cultivation of which it was capable; and it continued to improve as its commerce was extending itself to the immense limits within which it is now comprehended Whilst, by means of the advancement of its commerce, England became the grand magazine of all the riches of the old and new worlds, and of every branch and production of nature and art, its native tongue enriched itself in proportion to the national progress in trade, with all the helps and advantages derivable

from

from the language within the influence of
its correspondence, without varying from
its original genius and character   As it
was with its ancient rival, that the industry
of the nation has speculated with the greatest advantage to itself, in like manner it
has received the most benefit from the importation and introduction of her language.
To this rival the nation is indebted, not
only for an immensity of words and modes
of speech, which the language stood in
need of, but for that order, clearness, and
precision, which is so distinguishable in its
modern authors.   I do not mean, hereby,
to applaud any author who sacrifices truth
of sentiment and energy of thought to the
harmony of his periods

By the management of a master, whatever is barbarous and uncultivated in the
English language, becomes the source of a
number of the most perfect beauties Freed
from the shackles of grammatical rules, the
language admits of greater boldness and
variety in its style.   The value of this advantage is more perceptible in verse than in
                                    prose.

prose. Of all the poets, whose writings I have the happiness to read in their original tongue, the English appear to me to discover the greatest degree of grandeur, strength, and force in their compositions. The heart appears always to have dictated the most tender and passionate language in their poetry *.

It is surprising, that sounds so harsh and dissonant, should be rendered soft and melting, only by the force of sentiment, and by striking in unison with the tenderest feelings. When you make a comparison of these tender expressions with the natural phlegm of the English temper, will you not be inclined to believe, that love never

---

* I cannot here refrain from doing myself the pleasure of giving a specimen of this soft and tender language. It is taken from the tragedy of Venice Preserved, and is part of a speech of Jaffier to Belvidera.

O woman, lovely woman! Nature made thee
To temper man we had been brutes without you
There's in you all that we believe of Heav'n,
Amazing brightness, purity and truth,
Eternal joy, and everlasting love—

pleads

pleads his cause in this country till reduced
to the last necessity ?

The French language had been too
greatly honoured by the very extraordinary talents of M. de Voltaire, not to permit him the privilege of saying the worst he
could of it; he has, therefore, taken the
liberty of styling it a * *sturdy beggar* Yet,
notwithstanding this poverty, which he has
been pleased to reproach it with, this language has a fund of wealth justly belonging
to it, which is, an extreme variety of turns and
changes of expression.   I do not think the
English language can boast of so many.   It
may, by turns, be simple or sublime, majestic or trivial, serious or comical; but the
intermediate variations are, in my opinion,
not so easily marked out   Certain expressions, more or less noble, are not distinguishable by any particular change with
the same delicacy and severity. There are
either, properly speaking, no words or
phrases in English which are, in reality,

- The original is *gueuse fière.*

                                        mean ;

mean; or, if there really are such, they must be in great numbers, and the choice of them must depend entirely on fancy and caprice.

The particular facility with which the English are able to introduce foreign words into their language, has communicated to it an unpleasant kind of mixture, notwithstanding the pains which are used to bring the pronunciation to the proof of their own taste; and a nice and delicate ear cannot but be greatly hurt by a frequent discord, produced by the transition from one sound to another. May not Doctor Johnson's observation, on the style of Spenser, be applied in a great measure to the general character of the language? " He wrote (says " he) no language, but has formed, what " Butler calls, a Babylonish dialect, in it- " self harsh and barbarous, but made by " exalted genius and extensive learning, " the vehicle of so much instruction, and " so much pleasure, that, like other lovers, " we find grace in its deformity."

Johnson, with the elegance of style and

taste

taste for which he is so much remarked, has said, in his Life of Dryden, " this de-
" licacy of selection was little known to
" our authors; our speech lay before them
" in a heap of confusion, and every man
" took, for every purpose, what chance
" might offer him Those happy combi-
" nations of words, which distinguish poe-
" try from prose, had been rarely at-
" tempted; we had few elegancies or
" flowers of speech, the roses had not yet
" been plucked from the bramble, or dif-
" ferent colours had not been joined to
" enliven one another " What Johnson
has thought proper to say here of the authors who preceded Dryden, and his criti-
cisms on the works of that poet and his
successors, may, with very great justice, in
my opinion, be applied to English polite
literature in general

LETTER

LETTER XVI.

THE DINNER.

I MUST now give you some account of
one of the pleasantest days that I have passed here. On the evening preceding it, I
had orders from the Margravine to attend
her at Hammersmith, the next morning, at
an early hour, for what purpose I was not
informed I have often given you a description of that delightful spot If you
except Park-Place and Richmond, I believe few situations on the banks of the
Thames afford a more delightful prospect.
I found the noble large beech-tree next the
river, which conceals the view of the house
only to render the transient prospect of it
more charming, surrounded with tables,
decked out " * *with a princely magnificence.*"

---

* The words in Italics are of the author's introduction,

R

as

" *cence.*"   In a short time after my arrival,
I beheld a sight perfectly new to me, and
which made me think I was actually present at one of those splendid Venetian fes-
tivals, with which my fancy has been so
often charmed in description.   Neptune
was in the act of driving on the stream with
his trident—or, to speak like a common
man—it was the tide of flood when the
river was suddenly covered with boats and
magnificent barges.   The neighbouring
echoes were roused with the lively sound of
music, adapted to the occasion, which continued playing most delightfully until the
flotilla reached our shore.   At length, the
principal barge landing near the tree before-
mentioned, was saluted by a general dis-
charge of our little platform of artillery.
Amidst these confused sounds of cannon,
horns and clarinets, I observed about thirty
gentlemen, and more than twice that number

---

as are the others in this letter which are so distinguished,
and are taken *literatim* from the copy printed at Zuric.—
The Translator

of

of ladies, coming on shore, all most elegantly
dressed Their Highnesses preceded this numerous party and led it towards the tables
spread for the refreshment of the ladies and
gentlemen, who were now requested to place
themselves at the a There was, likewise,
a table set out for the six-and-thirty watermen who rowed the barge. These were
all uniformly cloathed, with caps and tas-
sels, white jackets, and silver badges, em-
bossed with the arms of the company they
belonged to Their table, as you may
imagine, was well supplied with liquors,
and they emptied their bottles very dex-
terously, amidst repeated *huzzas* When
the repast was finished, I was invited, with
the rest of the Margrave's court, to attend
their Highnesses in the principal barge, and
by the vigorous exertions of our spirited
boatmen, we soon passed the bridges of
Chelsea, Westminster, and Black-Friars.
The passage was so exceedingly pleasant,
that I thought it a very short one I passed
the time in conversation with the ladies
who sat next me, who were so polite as to

R 2 take

take great pains to understand me, as I on
my part did to make myself understood,
and amuse them.   The numerous villas,
gardens, and pleasant prospects which presented themselves on either bank, as our
well-loaded but nimble boat glided down
the stream, furnished sufficient topics for
discourse.   I do not think there is any ap-
proach to London which affords a grander
point of view than that which is seen after
passing Chelsea, on drawing nigh to West-
minster-Bridge   You then behold, in a
clear and extensive perspective, the dome
of St Paul's cathedral, and the steeple of
the church of St Martin in the Fields, two
of the most remarkable structures of this
immense metropolis.   Our barge stopped
on our arrival at London-Bridge.   Our
conductors here desired us to land, and led
us through a passage, not indeed a very
elegant one, into a noble and spacious
building, arrived at which, the ladies and
gentlemen were ushered into separate apartments   We were first conducted into a
large closet, in which were deposited our

hats

hats and canes; and certain very necessary accommodations were shown to us placed behind a large green curtain. These points being settled with all proper decorum, we were introduced into the court of assistants, and at last into the hall, where we were to be banquetted This room, which was very spacious, was more remarkable than any we had hitherto seen It was of a rectangular form, and regularly proportioned, of the height nearly of the saloon at Marli, the windows were towards the river, very lofty, and threw a clear and agreeable light over the whole hall The hall was itself encompassed by a very neat gallery It was capable of containing an assemblage of several hundred people It had at one end a handsome orchestra. After having viewed every part of the hall we rejoined the ladies, soon after which, dinner was announced to be on the table. Represent to yourself a table of the figure of a horse-shoe, placed in the middle of this large hall, with about one hundred and thirty or forty covers, the president of the

enter-

entertainment seated in an old-fashioned
state chair at the head of it.   On his right
hand sate the Margravine and her little
court, with the gentlemen; on his left his
own lady and the other ladies belonging to
the company   To give you, once for all,
an idea of a good English dinner, I must
inform you, that after some tureens of excellent turtle soup, as highly seasoned as the
cooks were able to send it in, came the
first course, which consisted entirely of the
choicest fish; salmon, trout, turbot, with·
lobster and other sauces.   The second
course consisted of game of several sorts,
particularly of buck venison, the fat of
which is so delicious, and this heightened
with currant jelly   The third course was
composed of tarts, puddings, creams, &c.
followed by a fine desert of every kind of
fruit which England could furnish, and
which really appeared very delicate; some
noble pine apples of exquisite flavour, excellent ices, and some of the best wines
which France and Spain produce   I must
not forget, in the detail of this dinner, its

respec-

respectable sideboard, which was an *English baron*, an immense piece of roast beef, placed on a table appropriated to the purpose, on one side of the hall, over which were displayed the colours of Great Britain. I was much diverted, during the time of dinner, with observing our waiters, who performed their office with much gravity of deportment and diligence of attention. They were three or four in number, and were beadles belonging to the company, who wore a clumsy sort of gown, the livery of their office. A still more striking object arrested my attention. It was a disagreeable figure, coarsely carved in wood, and painted, representing a man of a resolute hard-favoured countenance, holding a naked dagger in his hand. This colossus, as I may be allowed to style it, was placed in a spacious niche behind the president's chair; I was not at ease, after I had first espied it, till I was informed whom it represented. A person near me was kind enough to explain to me, that it was the statue of William Walworth, Lord Mayor of London,

R 4   and

and in his time belonging to the company
at whose hall we had the honour of dining
This Walworth, in the reign of Richard the
Second, killed, with his own hand, Tyler,
the leader of a numerous body of rebels,
who reduced the court, and city of London,
to great straits. The dagger with which
this eminent stroke of justice was effected,
has been carefully preserved, and is produced out of its scabbard upon occasions
like that we were celebrating From this
and other similar circumstances, you may
suppose, perhaps, that this magnificent entertainment was given by some ancient
order of knighthood. well, tell me, what
order you suppose it to be—it is certainly a
very ancient order, perhaps as ancient as
any in London, and one to which this
great metropolis, in all probability, owes
the foundation of its greatness, and in
which the first nobility of the kingdom, nay
kings themselves, and the princes of the
blood royal, have been ambitious to have
their names enrolled —You are at no loss
now to guess—I think you are; and I
must

must tell you it is the company of *fish-mongers*, that is to say, the dealers in fish, who enjoy certain very valuable privileges relating to the fisheries of the river Thames. It is one of the richest companies of the city of London, and the amount of its revenues is known only to a few of the members of it; but in all probability, it is not less than two or three millions of French money. The company is well known to have estates in Ireland of about sixteen or eighteen thousand acres of land It is further known, that this their great wealth is expended in the best manner possible. It is not wasted in good eating, but the greater part of it is employed in providing for the comfort and relief of the inferior classes of boatmen and fishermen, their wives and families, for the education of orphan children, and to afford succour and support to such members of their body as from old age, or misfortunes in trade, stand in need of it When the Margrave made a purchase of the charming villa and land which he possesses at Hammersmith, and

signified

signified a wish to be enrolled a member
of their body, the company not only readily complied with his request, but caused
a gold medal to be struck on the occasion;
on one side of which are the arms of the
company, and on the other the day and
year of admission, with this legend, *He
married an English woman*. *They adopted
him a brother* The chairman had been
upwards of two hours in conversation with
the Margravine, who discoursed him with
all that amiable and noble frankness and
affability so peculiar to her natural disposition, and which no communication with
courts or the world has been able to change
in any respect, when he begged permission
to leave his seat, that he might go round the
table to enquire how the guests had fared
He came to me amongst others, and said,
" *I hope you have made a tolerable dinner*."
I replied, that I had really never made a
better. After this ceremonial, several
large silver ewers were placed on the table
filled with rose water, in which the guests
dipped the ends of their napkins; (for at
these

these great entertainments the napkin is introduced as a luxury,) and I can assure you, this ablution after the eastern fashion, is one of the most refreshing that can be imagined. As it was known that the Margrave, though become a *true Briton*, is no friend to drinking, the *fishmongers* very politely declined promoting the drinking *toasts* In honour and remembrance of this day of festivity, we who were foreigners attending upon the Margrave, received, each of us, a small book elegantly printed, containing an exact list of the several sorts of fish taken in the Thames, with the times in which they are reckoned to be in season. Whilst we retired to drink our coffee in an adjoining room, the hall we dined in was decorated, as if by enchantment, and in less than an hour changed into a ball-room. The master of the company excused himself from opening the ball on account of his years, and his place was well supplied, as you will readily suppose, by the Duke de P——— and the Viscount de G———, who danced with much grace and ease. I had
the

the pleasure of seeing the wives, daughters
and nieces of these noble *fishmongers* dancing with Grandees of Spain, French Dukes,
and German Princes; and this charming
triumph of equality was the more delightful as it was conducted without any thing
that could scandalize decorum or good taste.
Great as was the pleasure I received from
this entertainment, and as much as I was
charmed with the Margravine's dancing,
who exhibited the graces and unaffected
dignity, one-while of a Heynel, another
time of a Guimard, I could not avoid joining company with a number of gentlemen
who had retired to a neighbouring room to
converse together over a bowl of punch.
I drank with them, and I endeavoured to
speak the best English I was able; and the
gentlemen were pleased to encourage my
efforts, by telling me they understood
what I said better than they did what was
spoken by the rest of the foreigners   The
topic of our discourse was, as may be supposed, peace and war.   Like most other
traders the *fishmongers* dislike the war   I
took

took the liberty of observing, that though war was a great evil, the situation of things rendered it unavoidable; that the injury which the trade and commerce of Great Britain suffered under, were, perhaps, occasioned not so much by the war itself as by the revolution which was the cause and rise of it; that their commerce derived a great part of its riches and splendour from the high estimation in which their political power was held within the two hemispheres, that in this world every thing had its certain value, and was to be purchased at its price; that a nation enjoying for too great a length of time the invaluable blessing of peace, became enervated, and without influence or resources, that the happiness of a great nation could only be secured by the greatness of its power and renown, and these it would not be possible to preserve without granting to its neighbours and allies all the assistance and support which the common interest of their governments required—I added, that I owned with the greatest sincerity in the world, that, though the

the present war was of all others apparently the most generous, and was now become the most necessary, it was, nevertheless, hazardous and burthensome, and England undoubtedly had done better to have prevented it, by offering its mediation at a juncture, when, in all probability, it might have been wished for, or, at least, such an offer treated with respect, and feared to have been refused. In suffering France to be ruined by despotism, whether native or foreign, England loses a rival necessary for her glory, and she loses, moreover, the richest consumer of a great part of her trade and manufactures. By securing to France a constitution consistent with reason, she ensures the downfall of despotism, and renders the empire of true liberty invincible.

With such conversation, trifling as it may appear, swallowing bumpers of punch or claret between whiles, we consumed the greatest part of the evening. The ball closed at midnight—supper was afterwards served, and we retired to rest in high spirits, but rather at a late hour.

LETTER XVII.

THE JOURNEY—WINDSOR—SLOUGH—OX-FORD—STOW—BLENHEIM

I HAVE lately made a journey of about two or three hundred miles through the interior parts of England, in company with that charming man, the Count de B——, the constant admirer of the famous Countess de Ros——, and the worthy M Rh——. If my pen were capable of giving you a faint picture of whatever was remarkable in the great variety of objects which presented themselves before my eyes, I am certain I should well amuse a few moments of your leisure. However, I can only offer you some slight sketches I will endeavour to present to your view our enjoyments in the same rapid succession they followed each other

Though we reached the beautiful terrace of Windsor by a gradual and imperceptible ascent,

ascent, I shall carry you up to it at once.
This terrace which is eighteen hundred
feet in length, appears to be high only
by reason of the vast extent of country
which is viewed from it. It is, perhaps,
the grandest and richest prospect that the
human eye has ever discovered :

> Here in full light the russet plains extend,
> There, wrapp'd in clouds the blueish hills ascend,
> E'en the wild heath displays her purple dyes,
> And midst the desert fruitful fields arise,
> That crown'd with tufted trees and springing corn,
> Like verdant isles the sable waste adorn.
> Not proud Olympus yields a nobler sight,
> Though gods, assembled, grace his tow'ring height

Notwithstanding what the poet declares
in these fine verses, to my eyes, wonderful
as this prospect is, it does not appear so majestic as those from our Alpine mountains,
though it includes the charmingly romantic view of the Thames winding its
course through the delightful vallies of
Richmond   An over-stretched prospect is
like unlimited power ; it has no relation to
any other thing, it fatigues the imagination
with-

without satisfying it, and the mind searches in vain for pleasures which may charm and command its attention.

The castle itself is only to be admired for its venerable antiquity, and the vast space of ground which it covers. You know well that it was founded by William the Conqueror. The whole building recals to mind the feudal times, and the age of chivalry Perhaps there are in no country of Europe more remains of feudal customs than in England. And further, there is, I believe, no country in which these customs are more happily blended with a system of liberty With these ornaments of ancient times the grandeur and majesty of the throne is constituted; but this grandeur and majesty, which serve to support and uphold the public force, is always consistent with law, and never in opposition to it.

There is little magnificence to be discovered within the castle The furniture is, for the most part, old-fashioned, worn out, and of a bad taste. It now contains some-

S   thing

thing of inestimable value, I mean the
seven cartoons of Raphael, which were
lately in the Queen's palace at London,
and formerly at Hampton-Court. These
noble designs on paper, and in water-co-
lours, have been carefully preserved The
idea of the artist is seen in all the freshness,
energy and purity with which it came
out of his hands I think if I were a
painter it would be from the study of these
inimitable works that I should form myself.
Invention by these models might best be
instructed how to improve and moderate
the fire of genius. From them the art
of painting may acquire all its mysteries
and resources St Paul at Athens is the
cartoon which pleased me most. What
judgment, what imagination, what variety
of composition! There are no two figures
which resemble each other; the air, the
posture, the manner of all are unlike. No
figure is out of its proper place, but each
forms the most natural, interesting, and the
justest harmony with all around it. There

is

is no single figure but possesses all the nature and dignity it is capable of

After viewing these noble paintings from which it was with much difficulty we could withdraw our eyes and admiration, we contemplated the pictures in the other rooms, among which, as you may well suppose, after those master-pieces, we did not find any great number that attracted our attention We took particular notice, indeed, of the chamber of beauties, as they were objects of curiosity. These are portraits finely painted by Vandyke of ladies remarkable for being the handsomest persons in the reign of Charles the Second. We saw Henry the Eighth by Holbein, undoubtedly an exact portraiture, but certainly a most terrific one; some pictures of Genario, whose works I had never seen before that I recollect, which appeared to be well designed, and finished with great delicacy. There was a piece of flowers in needlework by a modern Arachne which rivals the pencil of Vanspaendonck.

In the evening we went to Slough to
S 2   pay

pay our respects to the celebrated Herschel
He accepted of the appointment we made
with him to meet between the hours of
eleven and twelve at night Unfortunately
for us the night proved too clear To peruse the great volume of the heavens with
the most advantage, there must not be
much light; for it is a dark night only,
when the air is serene and calm, that is
favourable for celestial observations. We
therefore discovered neither churches nor
steeples, neither philosophers nor revolutions in the moon Mr Herschel convinced us only that there was no sea in that
planet, for what was hitherto supposed to
be water, appeared sensibly to our eyes to
be certain inequalities of surface casting
distinct shadows of more or less extent.
We ascertained with the greatest exactness
that what is generally called a double star
are two distinct ones, for they appeared
to be at a considerable distance from each
other. His observatory is a field, and his
telescope and the apparatus belonging to
it have the appearance at a distance of a
ship

ship of war. This enormous machine is, however, managed by him with all the ease and readiness of a common telescope. He assured us that the most skilful workmen in London could not fit up an instrument of that kind for thirty thousand pounds With this immense telescope, the speculum of which is of metal *, and if I mistake not magnifies an object to sixty thousand times its diameter, he has just undertaken a new journey into the heavens, which he reckons will not be finished in less than two hundred and fifty or sixty years As daring as this undertaking may appear to you, does it not seem to have

---

* It is an observation of M de la Lande that glass is a material of too confined a nature to be applied to this purpose, as, if it is over large, it is apt to bend, but a metal speculum may be wrought to any dimension, Mr Herschel having made one four feet in diameter This is capable of receiving an ocean of light, by which objects may be discovered that otherwise it may be supposed would have remained for ever invisible to human sight, such as the minute stars Of these the number seen through this telescope, which is forty feet long, is supposed to be from seven to eight hundred millions.

more

more consistency in it than the project of
certain philosophers who engaged to transport the whole race of mankind to the region of the moon in the course of three or
four of their tumultuous sittings? Mr.
Herschel is thought to be rather an ingenious mechanic than a skilful astronomer,
but it is not for one so ignorant of the science as myself to determine this point
His Majesty had ordered Mr Herschel to
construct a telescope like that with which
he made his famous discovery, and intended it as a present to the Empress of
Russia, but some disgust being conceived
against the Court of Petersburgh, for what
cause I know not, the instrument was not
sent to her Imperial Majesty, but is kept by
the King at Windsor for his own use

From Slough, we proceeded next morning to Oxford This is a small city in a
valley surrounded by little hills, well wa-
tered by a stream, and is an exceedingly
pleasant place Nature seems to have
formed here an asylum for the purposes of
a quiet enjoyment of the sweets of study,
and

and the steady pursuit of science and letters without interruption. The city itself
includes objects of peculiar singularity, for
here are huddled together twenty or thirty
piles of building constructed according to
various orders of architecture, the Gothic,
the Grecian and the Modern, all of them
very large, stately, and magnificent, at the
same time the adjoining houses are very
small, and built exceedingly plain. In the
streets you meet only doctors and students
in their black gowns with scarfs, some
more elegant than others; wearing caps on
their heads of a square flat form, with a
kind of tuft in the middle, which seems as
if it were the pin by which this little black
board was fastened to these learned heads,
or to these heads intended to be made so.

It is impossible not to be penetrated with
the deepest sentiments of respect for the
founders, at the sight of these noble monuments of the munificence of kings, officers
of state, and even private individuals, in
their zeal for the promotion of good learning; some from principles of gratitude,

others

others from motives of vanity, having chosen to immortalize their good deeds in the
most ingenious and striking mannei possible.   None of these noble colleges is
without a handsome libraiy belonging to
it, and some have collections of valuable
manuscripts, of fine paintings, and of natural history.   You may imagine I was
highly gratified with the sight of those famous antique marbles purchased by the
Earl of Arundel, and brought to England
in 1624.   They are at present deposited in
one of the rooms in the building called the
Public Schools.   Among these monuments
of the most celebrated epochas of Grecian
history, with what pleasure did my eyes
run over the dates consecrated to the dramatic triumphs of Eschylus, Euripides, and
Sophocles! In the same place are to be
seen the collection of marbles, and antique
busts and statues, presented to the university
by the Countess of Pomfret. These subjects are more valuable for their antiquity
than their workmanship; and some of
them are reduced to a state which renders

it

it difficult to discover what they were
meant to represent

There are several paintings of masters of
the Italian school in the magnificent college of Christ Church well worthy of observation   Amongst others there is a St.
John by Raphael, the vision of St. Francis
by Annibal Caracci, and several by Titian.
But of all the works of art of the greatest
importance here, because the performance
of national artists, is a representation of the
Christian Virtues in fix allegorical figures,
and the Holy Nativity, which ornament
the great window of the chapel at New
College   These are painted on glass by
Jervas after the designs of Sir Joshua Reynolds.   The middle group of figures appears to be something of an imitation,
though it is a happy one, of the celebrated
Night of Corregio   The allegorical figures
are very justly characterized; they are well
drawn and discover great taste and elegance.

From the manner in which I have
viewed this seat of learning it cannot be
expected that I should, from my own ob-
ser-

servation, undertake to inform you whether the education acquired in it, is equal
to the means it appears to me to afford for
that purpose   If I may be allowed to
speak after persons who have the opportunity of knowing the matter perfectly, education here, public as well as private, is
not so properly attended to as it might be.
There are fewer men of eminence for
learning at this time in England than formerly   It is a general complaint that the
professors are indolent and without emu-
lation, and that the students in particular
are negligent, and under no restraint   The
greater part of these are lodged in the town,
and lead most dissolute lives   It is noto-
rious that they keep mistresses, and that
students of inferior fortune club, two or
three together, to keep one betwixt them
Your philosophy would be much scan-
dalized to see in the refectories of many of
the colleges a table set apart for the son of
a nobleman, and this table more or less ele-
vated above the others   It must not, however, be forgotten, that the greater part of
these

these foundations are of remote dates, when the kings, cardinals, and archbishops, who were the first founders, had none of those sublime notions which the wisdom of later ages has inculcated It is further to be observed that a very religious respect is paid in this country to the will of deceased personages Ancient customs and practices are never altered here without the greatest circumspection

At Magdalen College we had the pleasure of seeing Doctor F , who appeared to be well acquainted with all our friends in France and Italy He is at this time employed in printing the Coptic text of the Scriptures This language, of which he knew not a single word two years ago, is become his principal amusement, as it is likewise that of his lady, who has undertaken to study it with him You will be under a difficulty, no doubt, to form any just notion of the gratification which this loving couple can derive from the study of Coptic The Doctor possesses great learn-

learning and knowledge, and is moreover
a most amiable and obliging character.

After having thus conducted you among
churches, colleges and libraries, I must
take you with me to the more delightful
scenes which are to be found at Stow, and
the gardens belonging to it—that Stow
which you know something of from these
lines of Pope.

> Time shall make it grow
> A work to wonder at—perhaps a Stow

I must afterwards lead you to Blenheim,
that proud monument of the gratitude of
a great nation for the services of a great
general. But I shall not undertake to give
you any particular account of these places,
which you will find fully described in the
views and guide to them which I bring
with me. I shall content myself with observing that, of all the gardens I have seen
in England, this of Stow appears to me to
be the noblest and best planned. It abounds
in erections of every kind, but all of exquisite taste; these are, a triumphal arch
which serves as the entrance to this beautiful

tiful place, three temples sacred to Peace, Concord, and Victory, the great Obelisk, Palladian Bridge, Gothic Church, Temple of British Worthies, &c The greater part of these buildings bring to the recollection the finest monuments of antiquity. The space within which they are included not being great, they might carry the appearance of being crowded together, did not the skill and judgment, shewn in their distribution, put it out of your thoughts. The intermediate spaces are so judiciously managed that you pass from one object to another with a degree of surprise; you only see each time what is intended to be shown you without any sort of confusion or irregularity. You may style it a fairy palace, if you please; or style it rather a spot chosen by the Muses for the consecration of glory, peace, and wealth, by an assemblage of every charm which rural nature, and the admired productions of the genius and arts of the several ages of the world have been able to produce.

You might think there is reason, perhaps,

haps, to find fault with some particular parts of this delightful spot. For instance, the black sand* at the bottom of the rivulet over which you cross to go to the Elysium has something too trifling in the idea, you would likewise disapprove of the church and imitation of a church-yard on the side of the lawn leading to the house I should think you would consider them as objects of too melancholy a nature, and therefore that they ought to have found no place here

Blenheim viewed from the gate leading from Woodstock, is one of the most striking prospects that can be conceived. You see at first a majestic river shaping its meandring course through an extensive park, and near you a charming little island, called Queen Elizabeth's Island; beyond it is a noble bridge thrown across the river; on one side that immense pile* of build-

---

* Blenheim was built by the celebrated Sir John Vanbrugh, and has obtained for him the following epitaph

Lie heavy on him, Earth for he
Laid many a heavy load on thee

ing,

ing, which enforces the strongest ideas of
grandeur and majesty from its amazing
mass of solidity, for it has the appearance
of a strength which would last to the remotest period of time *; and on the other
side stands that proud monument which is
consecrated by a grateful nation to the immortal name of its hero; I mean the fine
column on which is placed the statue of
the Duke of Marlborough in a Roman
habit with a pair of eagles at his feet, holding in one hand his general's staff, and in
the other a figure of victory This statue
is placed on a considerable eminence unconnected with any building, and seems to
command the large open country round it
In the midst of this display of glory and
greatness, the fancy is pleased to relieve itself with a view of the wood which once

---

* The author's ideas would, perhaps, have been best
rendered in the words of Dr Johnson, who, in one of his
letters, describes Durham Cathedral in this manner " it
" strikes,' says he, " with a kind of gigantic dignity, and
" aspires to no other praise than that of rocky solidity and
" indeterminate duration —Translator

con.

contained the bower where dwelt the tender Rosamond. It forms the back-gi ound
of the prospect, and the wood and spring
still bear the names so dear to young lovers
of Fair Rosamond's Bower, and Fair Rosamond's Well.

The garden front has the bust of Lewis
the Fourteenth which was taken down fiom
one of the gates of the town of Touinay.
Beneath the bust, and surrounded with iich
trophies, is to be seen the following in-
scription, as remaikable for its pomposity
as for its obscuity ·

Europæ hæc vindex genio decora alta Britanno.

What more particularly pleased me in
Blenheim park, was a giove of venerable
oaks, which, for their lusty vigour and great
antiquity, might well claim succession to
the oracles of the forest of Dodona; besides
these, the park abounds with magnificent
clumps of evergreens and shrubs, which
can be seen in no country except this, because in no other has gaidening been
brought to that perfection in habituating
the

the trees of every part of the known world
to its soil and climate, and in blending
and assorting the various tints of their verdure with such a charming effect.

Nuneham seems to be the seat of a simple individual in comparison with those
noble edifices of Stow and Blenheim, but
it might, perhaps, better serve as a model
for France or Germany   The plot of
ground which the garden occupies is of no
very great extent, and the erections are
plain and modest in their style, but at the
same time disposed with great ingenuity,
and in an agreeable taste   The subterra-
neous hotbed appears to me a contrivance
capable of producing charming effects, as
by its means the orange trees, and other
exotics appear in fine weather to live in
great harmony with the indigenous plants
and flowers.

I doubt if there can be a more remarkable
situation than Park-Place, a seat on the
bank of the Thames, in which every advantage has been taken of the singular
beauties afforded by its happy site.   There

you behold ruins of every sort, Greek, Roman, Gothic, and Egyptian; besides a
Stonehenge in miniature, the duplicate, if
I may use the term, of the most ancient
monument existing, perhaps, in Europe.
General Conway having discovered it by
digging in the island of Jersey, it was presented to him by that government; and
after a drawing made of it on the spot, and
every stone being particularly marked and
numbered, the General had it conveyed
across the sea with the utmost care, and at
a very great expence, and caused it to be
erected on this beautiful spot.

The General possesses an infinite deal of
taste for the arts joined to much information, and the most interesting frankness of
character and manners. His daughter has
sculptured a statue of his Majesty George
the Third in marble, which has been a
principal object of curiosity at the Museum
Leverianum, where are to be seen the best
collection of birds ever exhibited, with a
collection of uncommon articles brought
from the several places discovered by Cap-
tain

tain Cook, consisting of dresses, arms, idols, and utensils of every kind, together with the coat of mail which Cromwell wore when he defeated the royal army.

This noble collection, as you must have heard, was disposed of by way of lottery, and cost the actual possessor of it, I believe, one guinea only but never was fortune less blind in bestowing her favours than on this occasion; for the fortunate adventurer who gained this capital prize, possesses a great fund of knowledge, and a taste for natural history, and, accordingly, the collection has been much enriched by his pains and industry.

LETTER

LETTER XVIII

ENGLISH WOMEN---MORALS OF THE EN-
GLISH.

YOU have taxed me, my dear friend,
with negligence, for not having given you
a fuller account of the English ladies, and,
I confess, you have reason, we never can
say enough of them, at least when we
speak in their praise   For, if silence on
their subject be a certain mark of want of
breeding, to say a great deal concerning
them, for the purpose solely of degrad-
ing them, is, in my opinion, the greatest
proof of ill-manners which a polished people can be guilty of.

I told you, after my first voyage to London, that I fancied I observed a greater
number of handsome men than beautiful
women; but now that I have been in this
city during the winter season, when the
town has been exceedingly full, I must beg to
retract

retract this observation. I think there are
not to be found, in any country of Europe,
so many handsome persons of both sexes
as are to be seen here; I speak more especially as to the contour of face, that there
are no where such regular, or really perfect beauties This peculiar kind of perfection in beauty, calls to my mind a passage in Dr Johnson's works, which I have
often endeavoured to translate without satisfying myself in the task "To expand
" (says he) the human face to its full per-
" fection, it seems necessary that the
" mind should co-operate, by placidness
" of content, or consciousness of superi-
" ority" Indeed, it appears impossible
to have that perfection of beauty which the
English ladies possess, without that habitual
calmness and serenity of mind attending a
state of entire freedom from importunate
necessity, with an absolute command of
temper and happy disposition of mind and
character The people of this country
have features more fully delineated and
completely finished, than are to be met

T 3   with

with in France, Switzerland, or Germany;
female faces in particular, which are handsome, have great softness and delicacy.
If the over-scrutinizing observer thinks he
discovers any thing coarse or harsh in their
features, he finds it happily losing itself in
an air of suavity, which is not less distinguishable in their countenance than in that
characteristic calmness and dignity, without which beauty itself would cease to be
charming. It would seem as if nature had
only sketched out the features of the Parisian beauties, and left it to their coquetry to
alter and finish the work according to their
own taste; and this, perhaps, from caution, not to injure the happiness of a first
idea. I think I have now said enough to
convince you, that my admiration of English beauty has not made me forget how
agreeable our pretty women are; and with
what graceful and engaging vivacity even
the least handsome amongst them are able
to heighten and set off their charms.

England is greatly indebted to Sir William Hamilton for the acquisition he has
made

made of a considerable number of Etruscan vases and antique paintings, which is worth to the nation many millions annually, by the models and patterns it furnishes for the imitation in the several manufactures, as, from this collection, many very beautiful articles have been designed : but to what introduction or importation, or other happy conjuncture, this *expansion of the human face to its full perfection* is to be attributed I know not; the degree of perfection is, however, very apparent to my eyes. And, indeed, some Italians here, though highly prejudiced with notions of the superiority of their own country, have owned to me, that they did not think there were, throughout Italy, so many faces formed with a perfect symmetry, as are to be met with in London and its neighbourhood. This regularity of the features of the face, is certainly greatly heightened by the perfect whiteness of the skin. In this respect great advantages may well be supposed to result from the inconvenience of a cloudy atmosphere, and it may, perhaps,

be

be owing to this circumstance, that the human face possesses such a clearness of complexion *, as it is certainly fiom that cause that the gardens and meadows derive that charming verdure which is here so remarkable.

I cannot, however, help remarking, in this place, that English beauty is more striking than attractive At a distance you are charmed with its lustre, on a near aproach, you lament that it is not more lively and animated. The blood passes through those fine and delicate veins with moie calmness than passion, with more tenderness than love.

The common defect of these fine faces is, that they are somewhat too long; the heads have, however, the advantage of being well placed on the body. I cannot say the same of then shoulders; women in general wear stays very ill-shaped, which,

---

* The ardent orown, a colour of hair scarcely ever seen out of England or Scotland, greatly contributes to set off British beauty.

by

by pressing on the breast, occasion a
roundness of back and shoulders, and im-
pede the free motion of the arms, by forc-
ing them up too high and throwing them
too far back. And this is certainly an absurdity the more provoking, as you cannot
avoid readily perceiving that the women's
shapes are naturally formed with a capacity
of arriving at great ease and elegance;
which is evident, because they discover a
great deal of both under all the disadvantages of this ridiculous fashion. In general
their feet are large, and their legs rather
clumsy.

Here, you may, perhaps, be curious
to know my opinion, whether gallantry
prevails more in London than in Paris.
May I not ask, in my turn, what is your
opinion of this matter, after having considered what I have just now written? I have
taken the liberty of observing, that the
English ladies possess a style of beauty
which appears to have more calmness and
dignity than that of the handsome ladies in
Paris; but the latter have, at the same time,

more

more sprightliness and vivacity; the complexion of the former is more brilliant than
the latter, but less animated, their countenance more noble, and, perhaps, more of
the Roman, but less attractive and less voluptuous.   I should think, one of your
philosophical turn of mind might draw
more than one serious conclusion from
these premises.   I think it necessary to observe, that English women in general have
not full chests, and that the common sort
of people cover their bosom, as if unwilling
to shew it.   As to such women as have
chests well formed and really handsome, I
must remind you of what I have before
remarked, concerning these abominable
stays, which are absolute breast-plates, that
destroy this beauty, whilst they serve the
purposes of concealment and defence.
How often has virtue been preserved in
this world, by its being enabled to resist
the first onset!

You would do me, my dear friend, a
very serious piece of injustice, if you were
to suppose that I imagined these to be the

only

only arguments by which I support my opinion of the modesty of the fair sex in England. I know there is a great resemblance in the manners in great cities, and that immorality and vice spring up in every nation and amongst every people. But it is at the same time very true, that there are variations amongst different nations, as there are betwixt individuals of the same nation, and it is the office of the speculatist to discriminate these.

It cannot be denied, that the modes of living commonly followed by English ladies are very different from those of our countrywomen. In the first place, the sex is more separated, and converse more with each other. The interior œconomy of their houses, and the duties assigned their several domestics, are continual checks on their actions. In London, the office which is performed with us by a Swiss, or porter, is scarcely known. Visits are received only in a room on the ground floor. The lady's bedchamber is a sanctuary which no stranger is permitted to enter. It would
be

be an act of the greatest possible indecorum
to go into it, unless the visitor were upon
a very familiar footing with the family, or
did it upon some very urgent occasion.
There are impediments in the way of gallantry, which, however well-disposed a
lady may happen to be for an intrigue, are
not easily got over. Whatever may be her
quality, she must make her appointments
at some other house, either on her return
from a walk, from the play, or from a ball.
You see plain enough that what is brought
about with so much difficulty, cannot be
often put in practice, though, for the same
reason, more productive of pleasure and
satisfaction. I have already told you, that
men of genius only, in this country, possessed wit, in like manner, none but the
most abandoned women, or such as have
strong passions, are suspected of intrigue
and gallantry. The greatest difficulty is
not always to persuade an English woman
to suffer you to carry her off, but to find a
convenient opportunity for telling her you
wish to do it. Amiable and modest as they
are,

are, there is less art and good fortune required to bring the love adventure to a successful conclusion than there is to open it.

In England gentlemen employ all the time they can spare from public affairs, or private business, in the exercise of riding or walking, in the diversions of hunting or shooting, at the theatres, or in tavern clubs or societies At home a very small part of the long-sitting, sacred to the enjoyment of the pleasures of the table, is allowed to the female part of the family, and in which they can associate with gentlemen After the table is uncovered, and the small coloured cloths, which serve the purposes of napkins, are placed on it, when the bottles filled with Madeira, Burgundy, Claret, or Port wine, begin to circulate briskly upon the smooth surface of their highly polished mahogany tables, the ladies retire to their own apartment, and the gentlemen forget, sometimes altogether, but always for some hours after their retreat, that it is lawful to follow them

I have, to be sure, been present at routs and

and assemblies, which are meetings for the
purposes of dancing and playing at cards,
in which the sexes are intermixed. But
the ends of society are far from being answered by these kinds of meetings. You
will be surprised, when I tell you, that
these assemblages of good company are
only esteemed when they are the most numerous, and when subject to every inconvenience of a crowd So far from opportunities for conversation, it is a great chance
if you happen to meet with any person
you seek for and know to be present A
rout having been given in honour of the
Princess d'A——, it was so very brilliant
and magnificent that, the Princess coming
to it somewhat late, found it impossible to
make her way into the apartments of the
house, in which this splendidly aukward
entertainment was had on her account entirely.

The young Countess de N—— observed,
the other day, to the Duke of Queensberry,
that there was a great deal of show and
magnificence in London, that, indeed,

theie

there were many diversions and much amusement, but they were all, said she, of so dull a nature, so very dull——

It is, perhaps, descending too low, to attempt to characterize English female manners, by drawing examples from the most humiliated class of the sex. But, you know, variations are more immediately perceptible, and less liable to be mistaken in extremes. I am of opinion, that there are more common women in London than in Paris; from hence, I infer, that women of superior ranks less seldom interfere in these mysteries to which those unhappy creatures, through their own folly, or some cruel misfortune, have become devoted. And, what is no less remarkable, the priestesses of Venus here have more reserve and timidity, with a degree of decorum and even prudery, beyond any thing to be found amongst bacchants of our country.

I have to make, in this place, one observation, which appears a great contrast to my last remark. It is, that there are

many

many practices openly made use of betwixt
the sexes, which with us are considered as
marks of the greatest familiarity   On the
stage the actor applies his lips to those of
the actress, when he salutes her; the same
is practised by the people in general; the
kiss of love, and the kiss of friendship are
impressed alike on the lips   In the city,
suppers are usually closed with drinking
punch. The preparation of this liquor is
generally assigned to the female part of the
company, and it is thought a great mark
of politeness in a lady, to ask permission of
a gentleman to drink out of the glass which
he has just emptied   I was once favoured
in this manner by a very pretty young woman   If the rest of the company felt as I
did, upon the occasion, I presume the inconveniences attending a custom of this
kind would be soon discovered   In Paris,
we should be of opinion, that decency
ought to abolish this custom, especially as
the phrase which comes out of the mouths
of the ladies who make obliging proposals

to

to you as you go out of the theatres, is constantly, " *Will you drink with me a glass of wine* "*

Permit me now to dismiss the present subject, and close this letter with some observations of a more serious kind

I fancy that I have discovered, in the English nation, marks of a morality which, I think, seem not to be so discernible in France In this country, fathers, as well as mothers, pay great attention to their offspring, in the state of infancy Nothing is more common, in the streets and public ways, than to see the men performing the office of nurses and bearing children in their arms. The humanity and mild dis-

---

* These are the authors own English words The reader observes how grossly he has misconstrued the fashion at our tables, and the ceremony observed in drinking *hob and nob* From finding a similar phrase, in the invitation to it, made use of by women of the town, he has censured a very innocent practice —This should be a caution to English tourists, and writers of travels, how they deal out their censures, before they are sufficiently acquainted with the customs of the country which is the subject of their animadversions —The Translator

U   position

position of the lower kind of people is discoverable amidst all the confusion of their fu-
rious boxing-matches * These appear to be
conducted with all the noble generosity of
the ages of chivalry The combatants are
sure to meet with seconds, who encourage
and advise them, affording them every assistance they can have need of. The an-
tagonist who has received a fall in the contest, as I have observed in a former letter,
is never suffered to be attacked whilst lying
on the ground. If either combatant is
under the necessity of recovering his breath,
a knee is offered to him as a seat; one man
is employed in wiping off the dirt and
sweat, whilst another presents drink to
strengthen and refresh him. The two extremities of life meet here with the most
affectionate and respectful attention. As
there is here a greater degree of religious re-

---

* The author has introduced the word *boxes* into the
original, as an English word, but as we have, at present,
no such substantive plural in use in that sense, I have
changed it to *boxing-matches* —The Translator

spect

spect and regard (for such I would chuse to term it,) shown to young children when newly born, so likewise is there for deceased persons on their departure from this life; and these are, both of them, convincing proofs of the morality of a people. The dead are kept longer above ground here than in any other country of Europe It is seldom they are buried before the third day. The coffins, in which their remains are deposited, are framed with attention and great elegance. From the highest to the lowest classes, no funeral is conducted without a degree of solemnity. The man who has lived his whole life with the strictest attentention to œconomy, is liberal in the expences of a funeral The funeral car, or hearse, is stuck round with black ostrich feathers, two men walking before it covered from head to foot in black If it be the funeral of a single woman, or a man who has died unmarried, white ostrich feathers and white scarfs are used. The clergyman meets the corpse and conducts it into the church, and from thence to the place of

U 2   sepulture;

sepulture; the last ceremonies are accompanied with solemn prayers and exhortations. The burial places are preserved in neat order, and some of them form pleasant walks, where serious persons may indulge themselves in reflections and sentiments of piety and religion.

M. de Rh——, observed to me, a few days ago, that the English character appeared to him to be the German, ennobled by a spirit of liberty; and, from the nature of its climate and the effects of its extensive commerce and immense wealth, become less steady, more humane, and more easily excited to passion; at the same time, perhaps, more restless, dissatisfied and gloomy. From this influence of wealth and commerce it is, in my opinion, that an energy results, which is so extensive as to be out of the reach of calculation   Why is the soil of England so well cultivated ? It is because England is rich.   Why is England the seat of liberty ? Because it is a rich nation Why is the English nation so powerful ? Because it is a rich one.   Why does England

land at present pay so little regard to the attainment of arts and literature? Because England is too rich. With every advantage of an excellent constitution, of an improving system of agriculture, manufactures maturing to perfection, a flourishing commerce, and great strength by sea, with colonies well established, why is not England more peaceable and happy? It is because England is too rich *. because it has all the evils attendant on great wealth, and sets no value upon its advantages but as they produce riches. Physically and morally

---

* " Money," says Doctor Johnson, " confounds subordi-
" nation, by overpowering the distinction of rank and
" birth, and weakens authority by supplying power of re-
" sistance, or expedients for escape The feudal system is
" formed for a nation employed in agriculture, and has
" never long kept its hold where gold and silver has be-
" come common " One of the greatest mistakes made by
those who presided at the assembly of the States-General of
France was, their not being sensible of this truth , and, in
consequence of it, not perceiving that the third estate of the
kingdom was not what it had heretofore been, and that they
could not expect from it either the same virtues, the same
prejudices and compliances, or the same attachment to the
crown

U 3

con-

considered, gold is the sun of the nation *.
But is all the gold in the universe of any
worth when set in competition with the
rays of that luminary? A ray of the glorious and all-reviving sun disperses every
cloud, gives birth to flowers, ripens fruits,
warms the chill of old age, brightens and
exalts the charms, and the vivacity of
youth, and inspires infancy with harmless
mirth.

---

* Once on a time (the C de L said to me,) fate had a
mind to know what could be produced by indefatigable industry, and persevering study, with the magic of wealth, and,
after a succession of ages, this grand experiment displayed
all the wonders which now appear in the glory and prosperity of Great Britain

LETTER

LETTER XIX

FONTHILL.

The author, under the similitude of a dream, gives the Countess de V—— a description of the magnificent country-seat of William Beckford, Esq. in Wiltshire

I HAVE been, Madam, for several days under an enchantment, and should have forgotten all I had left in this world, if it were possible in any separate state of existence to erase you from my remembrance I beheld around me, as I fancied, every thing that I had before supposed delightful, every thing that I had once thought splendid, or had considered as charming, my imagination had nothing left to wish for, or desire; and these delicious sensations I enjoyed with a tranquillity the most pure and heavenly possible. I was one-while inclined to suppose myself departed out of existence; because, though naturally restless and active, I found I had no call to

U 4

use the least exertion My vision was not
disturbed on your account, for I considered
myself as preparing the way for your entrance into the Elysian Fields, where, I
fancied, you would speedily arrive.   I
waited your coming instantly, that I might
introduce you to the shades of the blessed
who surrounded me, and who, I hoped,
would love me the more when they found
I had had the happiness of enjoying your
friendship on earth

I will leave you, Madam, to judge for
yourself, whether I had not reason to suppose I had taken my departure from this
abode of sorrow which you inhabit.   I had
spent the most delightful evening possible
on the banks of the Thames, such a one
as I had supposed at one time could only
be enjoyed on the late fortunate banks of
the Seine.   At break of day I was taken
up by fleet coursers, and scarcely knowing whether I was asleep, or awake, followed in the train of a Prince, if virtue and
beneficence can confer such a title   He
was accompanied by a fairy, who consecrated

crated the whole power of her magical charms to protect him, and console him for the ingratitude of those on whom he had conferred benefits, or endeavoured to do so Had you seen her, you would have thought her to have been the **Queen of Sylphidia**: so brilliant were her eyes, so delightful and charming her air and shape. We crossed a wild country covered with heath and furze, as far as the eye could reach, we saw no appearance of that richness of cultivation which Albion boasts of, and of which travellers have given you such accounts *. One object, only, attracted

---

* There are, undoubtedly, many parts of England which are fully cultivated Of forests, the number is trifling, how otherwise would this country be habitable, which, being deprived of woods, is yet so very moist, did it abound with trees like France or Germany? At the same time what large spots are unproductive, being either converted into parks, or left in downs, and heaths! The uncultivated lands of the latter description do not altogether remain so because they are incapable of being made productive, but because some wealthy landholders derive considerable advantage, without trouble or expence, from the large flocks of sheep which are fed on them, whose wool fetches a great price,

tracted my attention for a few minutes during our progress This was an ancient
temple, whose ruins discover, from the
rudeness of the design, (which nevertheless
has an appearance of regularity,) and the
enormity of the masses of stone remaining,
that it owes its origin to the remotest antiquity. It seems incredible that man, such
as we ourselves are, should ever be able to
transport thither stones of that amazing
bulk, the like of which are not to be found
any where near it This stupendous monument is surrounded with small elevations
covered with turf, and some with a single

---

price, owing to the flourishing state of the woollen manu-
factories If you except Kent, and a few other counties in
England, there are not so many small landholders in this
island as in the provinces of France But I am well informed that to judge of the wealth of an English farmer,
we are not to be guided by the outward appearance of his
dwelling, which may be the means of forming a very erroneous opinion There are some farm-houses, and even some
manorial dwellings, which appear much out of repair, and
which are, nevertheless, inhabited by rich farmers, who do
not care to put themselves to the expence of keeping up
houses which are not their own

tree

tree, or small cluster of trees, such as are consecrated to departed souls. Every thing, therefore, round the temple seems to declare that in the early age of mankind this spot had been set apart as a burying-place, for a race of gigantic men or heroes*

My thoughts were still occupied with the objects I had been viewing, when I found we had reached the limits of the desart, and were entered into a charming valley, in which the Prince, and the Queen of the Sylphs, stopping, quitted their carriage at the gates of a palace, remarkable for the magnificence of its entrance betwixt four Ionic pillars, and the noble simplicity of the architecture of two wings of inferior height, which join the principal building

---

* Stonehenge There are five or six different opinions concerning the use and origin of this curious monument The most probable one, and the most generally received, is, that it has been a druidical temple Some antiquarians have maintained by many ingenious arguments that it was the burial-place of the first kings of Albion On the whole, it may justly be considered as one of the most ancient monuments of Europe

and

and become connected with it by two light colonnades of an elliptical form

This magnificent house stands in the middle of a plain of considerable extent, which is surrounded by several hills, the summits of which are some more distant than others, but all of easy ascents I never saw a happier variety of situations; the good king Solomon would have made a comparison of them with the graceful attitudes of his numerous concubines. One of these pleasant hills, cloathed with the thickest verdure, commands a wing of the house, and protects it from the westerly winds. The lovely green of the foliage unites with, and sets off in a very agreeable manner, the extreme whiteness of the stone with which this vast edifice is built. The other wing is bounded by a noble river, which winds slowly on, and having traced a number of meanders along the verdant plain, which it plentifully waters, forms a cluster of little islands covered with the most beautiful shrubs, and is at length lost in a thick forest, though which certain

vistas

vistas discover the distant prospect of a chain of richly cultivated hills.

You are not fond of descriptions of palaces, and fine houses; I shall not, therefore, give you any further account of this, though I know nothing of the kind in France of superior grandeur I shall not say a word of the elegant and rich apartments it contains, nor of the beautiful proportions of the gallery, the saloon, and the eating-room; nor take any notice of the paintings and statues which ornament them. I shall, however, accommodate myself to your taste by remarking that the fire-places have all of them noble jars of the rare old japan china, filled with all the gayest flowers of the season, which entirely occupy the vacant space As the weather was very warm we passed great part of the day on the ground floor, in a kind of Egyptian labyrinth, the recesses of which, ingeniously ornamented, contained besides other riches collected from every region of the known world, one of the most curious libraries I ever met with, furnished not only

only with the best books, but the best editions of those books, and, I may say, the
best and rarest copy of those editions

Towards the close of the day we were
attended by curricles drawn by little horses,
and driven by young postillions of a suitable size to the horses   These carriages
waited for us at the bottom of the great
steps, and seemed to be proper equipages
for the Queen of Sylphidia.   They conveyed us rapidly along the roads of this
maze of hill and wood; one-while descending with us into a deep valley; another time, mounting us up high hills from
whose tops we descried immense prospects, extending over several counties, and
bounded either by the sea or sky   These
views were continually changing to a new
country, and I thought myself by turns in
Switzerland, in France, in England, and in
America; now I fancied I saw a charming
landscape by Paul Potter, another time a
noble view by Claude Lorraine.

Having traversed a wood most beauti-
fully rustic, our conductors made a stop

at

at a rural gate which opened to us the moment we set foot on ground; and, in reality, I thought myself introduced into Julia's Elysium Following a path covered with moss, and bordered with beds of flowers intermixed with clumps of the most delightful shrubs, and of the wild laurel, the verdure of which is so pleasant to the sight*, we arrived at a small dome, which served as an entrance to a spacious grotto that had its principal front towards the river At the end of this grotto which has none of the trifling ornaments of shell-work, but seems constructed by large masses of

---

* I am much inclined to think that the plan of these delightful grounds was taken from the description given by Milton of Paradise in the following lines -

How from that sapphire fount the crisped brooks,
With mazy error under pendant shades
Run nectar, visiting each plant, and fed
Flow'rs worthy of paradise, which not nice art
In beds, and curious knots, but nature boon
Pour'd forth profuse on hill, and dale, and plain,
Both where the morning sun first warmly smote
The open field, and where the unpierc'd shade
Imbrown'd the noon-tide bow rs

rock,

rock piled together in a picturesque con=
fusion, a fountain throws out its chrystal
streams, which, falling with a gentle mur-
mur into a rustic bason, is conveyed under
the rock and mingles with the waters of the
river. As air is continually passing through
the two domes that serve as entrances, the
grotto is as dry as the best ventilated room
To increase our surprise, on entering upon
this enchanted scene, we found a table
covered with pine apples, grapes, and
other refreshments, in gold and china vases,
of the most exquisite shapes and workman=
ship.

At a small distance from this grotto is a
large cave, in which nature or art, for it
is not easy to discover which, has formed
several deep fissures, some having the appearance of cells, and others answering the
purposes of baths. The middle of this cavern is entirely open on the top, except
that a sort of covering is formed by the
shrubs which have planted themselves in
the crevices of the rock, and a fine tree
that seems to be planted by the hand of a
magician

magician in the centre of this retreat, springing out of a bed of violets bordered with green turf

We entered, in our walk, temples consecrated to various deities That which is dedicated to Hercules, is built on a small eminence almost disjoined from the other hills The temple of the Naiad, the guardian of this beautiful valley, is in a secret cavern, ornamented in the Etruscan taste, on the banks of the river with whose stream she waters it. The temple of Jesus Christ is at a distance from the boundary of these vast domains But I cannot help telling you, Madam, that these several buildings, without partiality to any one divinity, are greatly neglected The owner of this spot pays more attention to the remains of an ancient ruined tower, which has two caves of the most romantic appearance, one of them overgrown with ivy and vine trees, seems to be dedicated to the rites of Bacchus; the other is more awful and striking in its aspect, and, as it should seem, intended to celebrate the sublimest mysteries

X   of

of the institutions and wisdom of Fairy-Land·
but whether these mysteries are of a pleasing, or terrific nature, I am not able to inform you

Here, methinks, you stop me, and desire
to know what extraordinary being it is
that inhabits the spot I have been attempting to describe. You cannot ask me a
question which can puzzle me so greatly to
reply to The shortest answer I could
make would be to tell you that it is the
mansion of an enchanter And this, indeed, seems at first to be the best reply that
could be made; but then you would
scarcely give credit to it. In the first
place, I must needs own I never saw a being possessed of so great a share of wit, but
to wit, none of the Genii, you have ever
heard of, have any pretensions In the
next place, no being can be more amiable
or intelligent; and these too are distinctions for which this race is not remarkable,
because their power renders these qualities
unnecessary. When he touches the harp-
sichord, you fancy you hear Piccini, Gluck,

or

ór Orpheus himself playing on it. If he expresses himself in our language, he does it with all the genius and glow of Diderot, and the graces of Hamilton *. If he writes English, you would suppose it the only language he was acquainted with When he pleases to be eloquent, he has at command all the rhetorical powers of the English House of Commons †, and all the ar- tifice

---

* I have seen several works of Mr B's composition His Tales written in French are not more remarkable for easiness of style than originality of invention I believe of these only Vatteck has been ever published Than this, I know no eastern tale that is more in the oriental taste I never read any one which bears stronger marks of a preg- nant fancy and a peculiarity of manner, at the same time gloomy and terrific But his Letters on his Travels are, in my opinion, superior to his Tales They are in English , and, though printed, were never published The author has committed the whole edition to the flames, and has only preserved a single copy This work abounds with in- genious remarks and nice observations, the descriptions are warm and interesting, expressed in an animated and clear style, and strikingly exact

† The real character of the eloquence of the British House of Commons is, that of a perfect system of oratory.

Irony

tance of persuasion which the speakers in
your Convention possess   As an actor,
Thiemet

Irony is the figure most commonly used, and that in which
the speakers chiefly excel, and, perhaps, there is no other
which can be resorted to more productive of a certain and
speedy effect in arguments conducted with a degree of as-
perity and warmth   It is at the meetings of this assembly
only, that I have heard a question, as it is called, moved
and supported, then divided into its several heads, which
are separately debated in opposition   At other places, instead of do   s, I have only heard virulent speeches, and
loud reading, or lectures and orations previously composed,
and delivered with an appearance-more or less, of having
been committed to memory   In England, the real effects
of the party in opposition are seen, in the necessity the minister is laid under, of proposing such measures only as may
be able to stand a public discussion, and framing such prudent resolutions as may maintain their ground when opposed
by all the subtilty of argumentation, and ingenuity of talents,
which the dissenting party will not fail to bring against
them   One great advantage arising from this party-conten-
tion, on which the whole nation keeps a watchful eye, is,
that no one must venture to offer himself as a minister, or
the leader of a party, who is not conscious of superior abilities, and of powerful aids   A greater advantage still remains, which is, that no measure of consequence will be
adopted by the people's representatives, until it has been
considered in every point of view   and fully discussed in all
respects   A minister who should suffer a defeat in the
House

Thiemet and d'Albaret have scarcely greater talents With all these endowment, with all

---

House of Commons, in point of opinion, though he should still preserve a majority of votes in that house, would risk the loss of public favour, and could not long expect to maintain his influence in the Councils of his Sovereign

Of all the parliamentary speakers whom I have been able to hear debate, Mr Fox appears to me to wield the weapons of argumentation, and sometimes of sophistry, with the greatest force But, I think, Mr Sheridan possesses, in a superior degree, the component parts of perfect eloquence The vast stock of ideas with which his mind is stored, the choice which he makes of them, and the happy manner he has of displaying them, produce the most wonderful effects besides which, no one speaks with more elegance and propriety, or delivers his speeches more gracefully Mr Pitt's great talent seems to me to consist in a presence of mind, which enables him to produce such ideas as make for his argument, and artfully, to avoid such as are against it The strength of his oratory lies in the clearness and precision with which he brings back the most complicated discussions to their original object, and their real and decided result

There is no short-hand writer attending the debates in Westminster, as at Paris, or, I may rather say, the person who supplies the place of one possesses the whole art exclusively, in himself Without paper, pen or pencil, listening with closed eyelids, this astonishing genius, when returned home, writes down all he has heard, with greater

X 3

exactness

all that wealth is able to procure, I can assure you my enchanter is not a happy man.
An air of melancholy and regret obscures
the splendour which the graces of his person, and the gaiety of his temper throw
around him. I know well he has reason
to complain of mankind, and I think he
has cause of complaint against himself.
With the best disposition, and the most uncommon talents, spoiled by the gifts of nature and of fortune, his fancy must necessarily have become early vitiated Being
endowed with great strength and activity
of mind, objects were not easily found sufficiently interesting, and his imagination
was taxed with forming such as were dissi-

---

exactness than the speakers, whose discourses he has so
wonderfully retained, could do themselves.

[The readers of Parliamentary Debates, as given in the
news-papers, will not fail to recognise, in this portraiture,
their old friend Mr William Woodfall, who originally
began to detail them in a paper projected and conducted by
himself, and which, during the time he had the management of it, became exceedingly popular—I mean the
Morning Chronicle —The Translator]

similar

milar to what fortune had lavishly bestowed, and his most common notions became either terrific or whimsical; and were it not that his taste was just and refined, they would become more gloomy and fantastical —Of the many inconsistences with which he is charged, I have only remarked two, because they are such as suit least with my taste. -The first is, that he suffers flocks of geese and ducks to cackle and quack up and down that fine river, which ought to be occupied solely by swans The other, that he permits whole tribes of rooks and crows to blacken over the beautiful green lawn, on which are straying the peacocks that seem in waiting to be harnessed to the car of their divinity.

I do not know if my relation of the enchantments I have been under, have wrought any effect upon you, Madam; but it is high time that you were informed, I have been labouring to give you a description of the magnificent seat of Fonthill, in Wiltshire. Fully to

X 4　　　　　describe

describe all its beauties, it would have
been necessary to have invoked the shade
of Gessner, or the genius of *Paul and Vir-
ginia*, in one of the rural and poetic caves
I have before noticed   The owner of this
noble estate is Mr B—, one of the richest
individuals in Europe   The immense fortune which he is in possession of is derived
from one of his ancestors, who shared the
glory of the conquest of Jamaica, which
Columbus had made the magazine of all
the riches he brought from the new hemi-
sphere he had discovered, whether for the
advantage or disadvantage of the human
race, I shall not determine   What he possesses in that island only, will, this year
produce to him, upwards of one hundred
thousand pounds   The land about Fonthill, which is only a small part of what he
owns in the adjoining county of Somerset,
is laid out entirely in a pleasure-ground,
containing from sixteen to eighteen hundred acres. Mr. B. is very sensible that
great land-holders like himself are prejudicial to a country, he endeavours, therefore,

fore, to compensate for the injury fortune forces him to do, by furnishing constant employment for four or five thousand labourers, who are all in his pay. He is the proprietor of the town of H—, which sends two members to Parliament, the choice of which you undoubtedly guess, is regulated by him. At the last election, one of the members, willing to shew his gratitude for the loud acclamations of the electors, began an eloquent harangue, which was interrupted by one of the electors, who entreated him to spare himself the trouble of returning thanks. " for," added he, " if the *squire* had sent his " *great dog* to us, we should have chosen " him, as we have done you."

The mental powers which Mr B. is possessed of, perhaps, as much exceed all example as does his fortune. Wonderful as his genius appears, it is a question, whether, from indolence, or from whatever other secret cause, he has advanced to the midway of that excellence which nature seems to have designed him to attain. besides, he

is not more than three-and-thirty years of
age *.

---

* The Translator, who has experienced Mr B 's libe-
rality and bounty upon the occasion of introducing this
translation to the public, being under an injunction of making any acknowledgment by way of dedication, cannot
help obeying the dictates of his gratitude in this note,
though he may thereby hazard Mr B 's displeasure

LETTER XX.

THE COUNTESS DE V——'S ANSWER TO THE FOREGOING LETTER *.

HOW sensibly am I affected by your kindness in sending me that charming letter, and sparing so much time from the enjoyment of those visions of delight, that I might be a partaker of your pleasures! —I am much deceived if the description does not dwell longer in my recollection than the sight will in yours, extraordinary as may be the enchanter, and his palace too. If I mistake not, the magician who

---

* There are several compliments paid me in this letter, indeed, so many, that it might seem to have been more modest to have suppressed the letter altogether but I could not prevail on myself to do it, so much am I charmed with the tender friendship of the writer I have, therefore, come to a resolution rather to expose myself to the censure of the critical reader on this account, than deprive him of a letter which pleases me more than any thing I have to offer besides to his perusal.

possesses

possesses exclusively so large a part of this
globe, has made some trials of his art in
this place I think I have met with ladies
who were enchanted at some of his ban-
quets, and I was once very much impor-
tuned to be present at them. There was,
at that time, a talk of a temple with myste-
rious rites. I obtained, for others, the
liberty of celebrating them; I was happy,
then, in my retirement, and I pitied those
who could not enjoy in solitude the same
hopes and reflexions as I did —I can only
set you upon thinking, and I ought to
have every expectation of finding favour
from one who gives up the enjoyments
which suspend his dissatisfaction in order
to relieve me from the mortifications which
he judges I labour under I never had
but one delightful dream in my life, and I
will relate it to you—though, in so doing,
I may chance to make you fall asleep

Worn out, one evening, with care and
solicitude, and dreading to seek repose, as
for several months sleep had forsaken my
eyelids, I chanced to lay my hand on a
col-

collection of prints Turning them care-
lessly over, one happened to excite my attention above the rest. It was a print of
Saint Jerome sleeping in the desart, surrounded by tigers. If the scene has the
effect of making the beholders shudder, the
countenance of the holy man is sufficient
to restore tranquillity His soul seemed
wrapt in a heavenly vision, such as every
being would wish to enjoy I laid me
down with regret that I could not hope so
much, and late for the first time granted
me my secret wish Scarcely were my
eyes closed, when I thought I was taken
by the hand, and softly accosted by the
name I had been accustomed to hear myself called in my infancy I should have
been frightened had not the voice dissi-
pated my fears An agreeable light appeared in my room, and by it I distinctly
beheld my father sitting by my bed-side
Joy and surprise, on seeing again the object of my tenderness and regard, deprived
me of utterance But, as souls released
from the body know what passes in our
minds,

minds, he *saw* immediately my thoughts:
" It is on your account," said he, " that
" I have quitted the mansions of bliss, and
" come to pass a few moments in these
" regions of vice and misery. Whilst I was
" living, it was matter of great concern to
" me to find that you were not happy,
" now that I am in the shades below, your
" sufferings interrupt my bliss I have
" permission from heaven to visit you be-
" fore you join me in my state of eternal
" rest, to console your mind, and enlighten
" it respecting the future "---I could wish
that he had imparted to me his eloquence,
as I could then have explained to you the
many comfortable and tender expressions
he made use of. I did not waste time in
giving him the sad history of events with
which he was well acquainted—his apparition convincing me of the truth of the
immortality of the soul, I pressed him to
discover the secrets of a future existence.
He replied to all my enquiries very satis-
factorily. But, though spirits may be
able to resolve all the doubts and difficulties

of

of the profoundest metaphysics, it is not
for mortals to retain in memory, these sublime truths   There have, indeed, been
some few persons endowed with powers of
genius sufficient to have gained some slight
apprehension of them, and your writings
lead me to think you are of that number
I can, now, only call to my recollection,
his description of the blessed mansions, and
his account of the manner after which he
passed his time in Elysium   With some
few variations, your details agree with his
relation of that heavenly place   The aver-
sion they retain for whatever was the cause
of their corruption upon earth, makes them
avoid the use of golden vases   Their nectar and ambrosia, and such fruits as you
partook of in the enchanted cave, are
served to them in vessels of chrystal   He
made mention to me of no Sylphid, but he
had near him my daughter and the female
friend who preceded him   The one made
a part of his delight by day, the other discoursed him frequently on my love and regard ; and anticipating the genius charged
with

with the news of this world she told him
every thing he might wish to know; and
as she preserved all the curiosity of her
years, and the satisfaction she found in telling all she knew, she did not fail to inform
him of every incident that befel me   He
told me, that a portion of their time, in these
regions of bliss, was employed in an attention to those whom they expected to
meet there.   As long as these continue
sojourners on earth, they erect funeral
monuments for them, which they decorate
with branches of poplar, willow, and cy-
press, and invoke the gods in their favour;
but, when they learn news of their speedy
arrival, they prepare a dwelling-place for
their reception, agreeable to their tastes
They adorn these retreats with garlands of
flowers; but, if the genius of celebrity attends them on their journey, they inter-
weave crowns of laurel with the flowers
It appeared, from what he said, that we
were far from being cold or insensible in
this state of repose, but quite different from
what we find in this world; happiness was
caused

caused by a susceptibility of experiencing
every feeling and passion, followed by no
ill-consequence, their excess only being
unknown   You will easily believe me,
when I say, that I used many pressing instances to be allowed to accompany him
and quit this abode of sorrow.   He answered me only by pointing to the bed on
which my mother was sleeping   As the
time advanced, and, as doubtless, he perceived the moment of separation would
prove painful to me, he called my attention to the description of the only temple
which existed in Elysium   It is consructed
with the magical power of appearing to
every inhabitant of Elysium, in the form,
and with the ornaments he is best pleased
with   To such as, like him, are pleased
with simplicity, the statue of Happiness
only appears   At the farther end of the
sanctuary and at the feet of the Divinity, a
gentle flame is seen burning, and has been
so from all time   Spirits are continually
employed in supplying this flame, by
throwing on it the leaves of a plant un-

Y   known

known upon earth   This is the whole
worship paid to the goddess   If they neglect this task, a kind of languor creeps upon
them and robs them of their enjoyments,
which, as you may readily suppose, they
are eager to send amongst us   The temple
is of that vast extent that every spirit has a
niche to itself, which it visits daily   In
this niche, and at the further end of it, over
an altar, is hung a canvass frame of an oval
shape   On the altar is a vase filled with
perfumes.   Whenever we, who remain
here upon earth, honour the memory of
these departed spirits, by raising some monument of our friendship and esteem, the
incense burnt here reaches the altar, and
the perfumes on it take fire, the ethereal
vapour from which arises to the magic
frame, and impresses on it the likeness of
the person by whom this mark of respect
is shown.   This picture is disposed of by
the spirit thus honoured, amongst the dear-
est companions of its blessed existence.
Heretofore there was a necessity for each
spirit continually to renew this magic frame,

on

on account of the high respect formerly
shown to departed spirits, arising from filial
regard, or public or private gratitude, virtues
which exist now in remembrance only But,
for many years past, the only sentiments
which these niches present are, those of im-
pious neglect and base ingratitude, sentiments
which, even in Elysium, are found to be
painful My father concluded his narration with these words " Since," said he,
" I have been separated from mortal life,
" my perfumes have only taken fire once;
" but that has been sufficient for my com-
" fort. I have brought with me the im-
" pression made by it on the frame, and
" you will easily discover to whom it be-
" longs " So saying, he presented me
with a drawing, which I examined atten-
tively with my eyes, and found out the
resemblance I then thought I heard the
beating of a drum, and that Discord, with
the furies in the train of that demon, entered my chamber I placed the portrait
close to my breast, that it might not be
polluted by these demons breathing on it,

and

and I awoke   All that remained was this portrait, and the recollection of my dream: I send you the latter, and you will find, on your return, the former placed in your bed-chamber.   I learned, the day before yesterday, that you had broken your arm; all my delightful visions are fled, care and anxiety are redoubled, and you are, as I think, for evermore preserved from such tedious dreams,

THE END

BOOKS

PRINTED FOR

T N LONGMAN AND O REES,

No 39, Paternoster-Row

1 The LIFE of CATHARINE II Empress of Russia The Third Edition, with considerable Improvements In Three volumes, 8vo Price 1l 4s in Boards Embellished with Seven elegant Portraits, and a correct Map of Russia

To the concurrent testimonies of all the periodical publications of taste and literature already adduced, we shall only add, from the European Magazine, that the writer of their Review after delaying his account of the Work, in order to ascertain its authenticity, in the Number for November last, says " On the most indisputable testimony, and the highest authority, the writer has it now in his power to declare, that these volumes, under the modest and limited title of ' The Life of the late Empress of Russia comprise a faithful and impartial History of the Political Transactions and Public Affairs of the Northern Courts of Europe, during the Reign of Catharine II , together with a regular narration of the progressive aggrandizement, civilization, and general improvement, of the Russian Empire, from the time of Peter the Great to that of the death of the late Empress in 1796 '

2 BIOGRAPHICAL, LITERARY, and POLITICAL ANECDOTES, of several of the most EMINENT PERSONS of the PRESENT AGE, particularly the Dukes of Grafton, Leeds, Dorset, and Rutland, Lords Townshend, Orford, Marchmont, Mansfield, Camden, Temple, Nugent, and Sackville, Bishops of Hereford and Ossory, Right Hon George Grenville, Charles Townshend, Sir James Caldwell, Sir Grey Cooper, Sir John Dalrymple, Serjeant Adair, Dr Franklin, and many others, never before printed In Three Volumes Price 18s

The writers of the Monthly Review say " We cannot dismiss these volumes without observing, that they contain a considerable portion of political information The work will, by its discerning readers, be characterized as highly interesting and it will prove particularly so to those who still remember the times to which the anecdotes here recorded are referable To the future historian also it will afford much assistance, by contributing, in many instances, towards the means of information, which, but for publications of this kind, might be utterly consigned to oblivion '

3 The ANECDOTES of LORD CHATHAM'S LIFE The Sixth Edition In Three Volumes, 8vo Price 18s Boards

" The author has made a valuable collection of Anecdotes, especially of the late and most conspicuous part of Lord Chatham's Life, and of other matters connected with it He says he i not conscious

of

of having advanced one falsehood, we give credit to his declaration, having found no cause to doubt ;

Monthly Review, May 1792

' A greater number of curious and interesting Anecdotes, concerning public affairs, have not appeared since the days of Sir William Temple, than are to be found in this work

" We cannot dismiss this article without acknowledging, that it throws a great and new light upon the occurrences and events of more than half a century of our history

Gent Mag Aug 1793

4 A RESIDENCE in FRANCE, during the Years 1792, 3, 4, and 5, described in a series of Letters from an ENGLISH LADY, with general and incidental Remarks on the French Character and Manners Prepared for the Press by JOHN GIFFORD, Esq In Two Volumes, 8vo Price 14s Boards The Third Edition

" It is only justice to say, that the style is as polished as the matter is interesting and important, nor have we any doubt that the book will remain a permanent monument of the taste and talents of the writer *British Crit c, April* 1797

5 GLEANINGS THROUGH WALES, HOLLAND, and WESTPHALIA, with Views of Peace and War at Home and Abroad To which is added, HUMANITY, or, The Rights of Nature A Poem Revised and corrected By Mr PRATT In Three Volumes, 8vo Price One Guinea in Boards The Third Edition

" We have found so many lively and pleasant exhibitions of manners, so many amusing and interesting anecdotes, and so many observations and reflections, gay and grave, sportive and sentimental, (all expressed in a gay and familiar style,) better suited to the purpose than sentences laboured with artificial exactness, that we cannot but recommend it to our readers as a highly amusing and interesting performance " *Analytical Review, Jan* 1796

6 JOAN of ARC, an EPIC POEM By ROBERT SOUTHEY Handsomely printed on fine Wove Paper, and Hot pressed, in Two Volumes, Foolscap 8vo Embellished with an elegant Portrait of the Maid of Orleans The Second Edition Price 12s Boards

7 LETTERS written during a Residence in SPAIN and PORTUGAL By ROBERT SOUTHEY Price 7s in Boards

" In the variety of amusement which Mr Southey has served up in this Melange, the mind is at a loss on which page mostly to dwell —Relying on our author's assurances, we must think him either a very fortunate or a very inquisitive traveller, he must either have been unusually lucky in meeting, fortuitously, with adventure and information, or have spent many a weary hour in the research, for

not

not a page occurs that does not either amuse us by its humour, or instruct us by a just train of thoughts happily expressed

London Review, March 1800

8 A NEW VOLUME of POEMS, by ROBERT SOUTHEY, printed on fine wove paper Price 5s Boards

9 FAMILY SECRETS By Mr PRATT In Five large Volumes, 12mo Price 1l 5s Boards Second Edition

" Mr Pratt has introduced to a set of numerous readers a Novel that has the merit of being at once tender, pathetic, and full of love and, which may be a more uncommon circumstance, of love mixed with the greatest discretion '

Monthly Review, May 1797

10 A GOSSIPS STORY and LEGENDARY TALE By Mrs WEST, Author of Advantages of Education, &c In Two Volumes, 12mo Price 7s in Boards Third Edition

" We can recommend this story as uniting to a great degree of interest the rarer qualities of good sense, and an accurate knowledge of man kind The grammatical errors and vulgarisms which disgrace many even of our most celebrated novels, have here no place, and several of the shorter poetical pieces interspersed through the work have very considerable merit Amusement is combined with utility, and action is enlisted in the cause of virtue and practical philosophy '

Monthly Review, Jan 1797

11 A TALE of the TIMES By the same Author In Three Volumes, 12mo Price 12s sewed

12 ANECDOTES of TWO WELL-KNOWN FAMILIES Written by a Descendant, and dedicated to the first Female Pen in England Prepared for the Press by Mrs PARSONS In Three Volumes, 12mo Price 10s 6d in Boards

13 AN OLD FRIEND WITH A NEW FACE, a Novel By Mrs PARSONS In Three Volumes, 12mo Price 10s 6d in Boards

14 OCTAVIA By ANNA MARIA PORTER In Three Volumes, 12mo Price 10s 6d in Boards

15 The FALSE FRIEND, a Novel By Mrs RO-BINSON In Four Volumes, 12mo Price 10s sewed

16 RASH VOWS Translated from the French of Madame GENLIS In Three Volumes, 12mo Price 10s 6d Boards

" To such of our readers as are acquainted with the writings of Madame Genlis, it will be almost unnecessary to say, that the precepts

cepts she inculcates are those of wisdom and virtue In this, as in her former works, she displays an acquaintance with all the varieties of the human character, which she happily discriminates
London Review 1 eb 1799

17 The NATURAL SON Translated from the French of DIDEROT, Author of James the Fatalist, the Nun, &c In Two Volumes, 12mo Price 7s Boards

" The style of his work denotes the hand of a master, and the translation is much better than we are accustomed to meet with in works of this nature

" The Novel, as it appears in its English dress, strongly tends to cherish the best feelings of the human heart, and on the whole, there are few readers who will think a leisure hour ill-bestowed on the perusal of the letters of this Natural Son
London Review, Feo 1799

18 The SPIRIT of the ELBL, a Romance In Three Volumes, 12mo Price 9s Boards

---

In the Press,

And speedily will be published, in Three Volumes, 8vo

1 A VIEW of the RUSSIAN EMPIRE, during the Reign of Catharine the Second and to the Close of the present Century By the Editor of the Life of Catharine II

---

2 TRAVELS of ANTENOR in GREECE and ASIA, with some Ideas upon Egypt Translated into French from a Greek Manuscript, found at Herculaneum, by E F LAUTIER, and now from the French into English

---

3 TRAVELS through the SOUTHERN PROVINCES of the RUSSIAN EMPIRE Translated from the original German of Professor PALLAS, Counsellor of State to the Emperor of Russia Member of the principal Literary Societies of Europe, &c &c By A F M WILLICH, M D and STEPHEN PORTER, of Trinity College, Cambridge, Esq In Two Volumes, 4to embellished with near one hundred coloured Plates and Maps, illustrative of the Manners, Dress and Customs of the various Tartar Nations, and of different Subjects relative to the Natural History and Antiquities of a Tract of Country, extending several thousand Miles in length, and never before described Price about Six Guineas

*** A few Copies of this splendid Work will be printed on fine Royal Paper with proof Impressions of the Plates

CPSIA information can be obtained at www.ICGtesting.com
Printed in the USA
LVOW031941220712

291073LV00014B/68/P